Northu
the Borders *and*
Hadrian's Wall

WALKS

Compiled by
John Brooks,
Brian Conduit
and Hugh Taylor

JARROLD
publishing

Acknowledgements

We would like to thank the Countryside Department of
Northumberland County Council for help in checking rights of
way and Mr A.F. Jones, Hexham, of the Ramblers' Association
for his help in checking amendments to routes. We are also
grateful for the invaluable assistance that we have received
from the Scottish Borders Tourist Board, Borders Regional
Council, Scottish Natural Heritage and local tourist information
offices. The publishers also thank Mr Graham Taylor (Chief
Executive) and Mr Neil Diment (Senior Interpretive Services
Officer) of the Northumberland National Park Authority, who
provided the text on page 13.

Text:	John Brooks, Brian Conduit, and Hugh Taylor
Photography:	Jarrold Publishing, Brian Conduit
Editor:	Sonya Calton
Designers:	Brian Skinner, Doug Whitworth
Series Consultant:	Brian Conduit

OS Ordnance Survey This product includes mapping data licensed
from Ordnance Survey® with the permission of
the Controller of Her Majesty's Stationery Office. © Crown
Copyright 2003. All rights reserved. Licence number 100017593.
Ordnance Survey, the OS symbol and Pathfinder are registered
trademarks and Explorer, Landranger and Outdoor Leisure are
trademarks of the Ordnance Survey, the national mapping
agency of Great Britain.

Jarrold Publishing   ISBN 0-7117-1088-0

While every care has been taken to ensure the accuracy of the
route directions, the publishers cannot accept responsibility
for errors or omissions, or for changes in details given. The
countryside is not static: hedges and fences can be removed,
field boundaries can be altered, footpaths can be rerouted and
changes in ownership can result in the closure or diversion of
some concessionary paths. Also, paths that are easy and
pleasant for walking in fine conditions may become slippery,
muddy and difficult in wet weather, while stepping-stones
across rivers and streams may become impassable.

If you find an inaccuracy in either the text or maps, please
write to Jarrold Publishing at the address below.

First published 2000, 2003
by Jarrold Publishing

Printed in Belgium
by Proost NV, Turnhout 3/03

Jarrold Publishing
Whitefriars, Norwich NR3 1TR
E-mail: info@totalwalking.co.uk
www.totalwalking.co.uk

Front cover: Hadrian's Wall from Peel Crags
Previous page: Dunstanburgh Castle

Contents

The National Parks and Countryside Recreation; The National Trust; The Ramblers' Association; Walkers and the Law in England and Scotland; Countryside Access Charter; Safety on the Hills; Useful Organisations; Ordnance Survey Maps

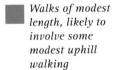

Short, easy walks

Walks of modest length, likely to involve some modest uphill walking

More challenging walks which may be longer and/or over more rugged terrain, often with some stiff climbs

Keymap 1

Keymap 1

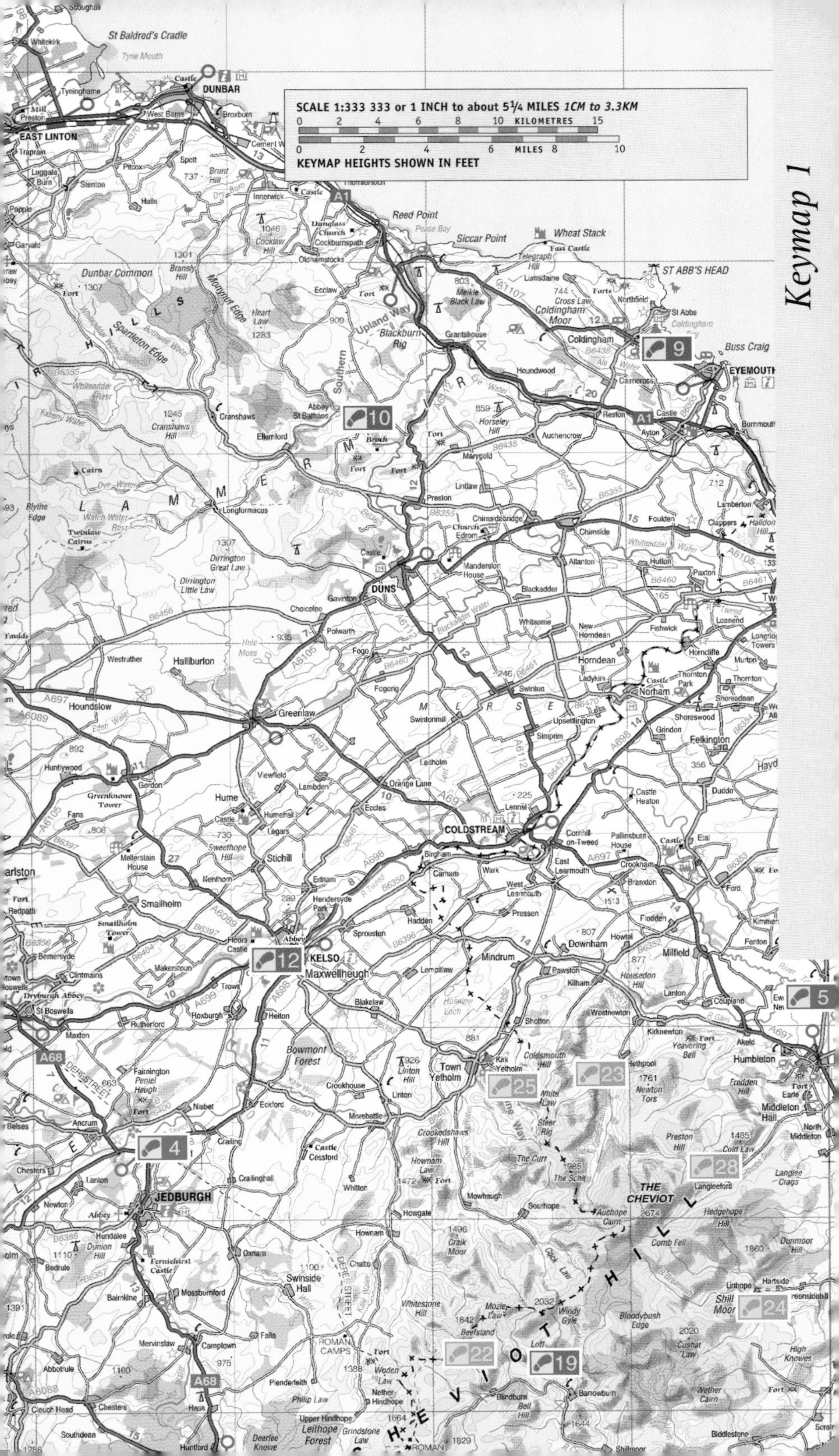

SCALE 1:333 333 or 1 INCH to about 5¼ MILES 1CM to 3.3KM
0 2 4 6 8 10 KILOMETRES 15
0 2 4 6 MILES 8 10
KEYMAP HEIGHTS SHOWN IN FEET
St Baldred's Cradle
Tyne Mouth
Whitekirk
Tyninghame
DUNBAR
Castle
West Barns
Broxburn
EAST LINTON
Traprain
Luggate Burn
Stenton
Pitcox
Spott
Brunt Hill
Halls
Innerwick
Castle
Reed Point
Pease Bay
Siccar Point
Wheat Stack
Fast Castle
Telegraph Hill
Dunglass Church
Cockburnspath
Oldhamstocks
Cocklaw Hill
Bransly Hill
Dunbar Common
Monynut Edge
Spartleton Edge
Heart Law
Ecclaw
Fort
Upland Way
Southern
Blackburn Rig
Meikle Black Law
Lumsdaine
Cross Law
Coldingham Moor
Coldingham
ST ABB'S HEAD
Northfield
St Abbs
Buss Craig
EYEMOUTH
Grantshouse
Houndwood
Cairncross
Reston
Ayton
Burnmouth
Whiteadder Resr
Cranshaws
Cranshaws Hill
Ellemford
Abbey St Bathans
Broch
Horseley Hill
Auchencrow
Marygold
Lintlaw
Preston
Cairn
Dye Water
Blythe Edge
Watch Water Resr
Twinlaw Cairns
Longformacus
Dirrington Great Law
Dirrington Little Law
Chirnsidebridge
Church Edrom
Chirnside
Foulden
Lamberton
Clappers
Halidon Hill
Whiteadder Water
Allanton
Hutton
Paxton
Manderston House
Castle
DUNS
Gavinton
Blackadder
Choicelee
Polwarth
Hule Moss
Fogo
Blackadder Water
Whitsome
New Horndean
Fishwick
Loanend
Horndean
Horncliffe
Ladykirk
Norham
Thornton Park
Thornton
Westruther
Halliburton
Fogorig
Swinton
Houndslow
Greenlaw
Eden Water
Swintonmill
Upsettlington
Shoresdean
Shoreswood
Grindon
Felkington
Simprim
Leitholm
Huntlywood
Gordon
Greenknowe Tower
Hume
Viewfield
Lambden
Orange Lane
Castle Heaton
Duddo
Fans
Castle
Humehall
Legars
Eccles
Lennel
COLDSTREAM
Cornhill-on-Tweed
Pallinsburn House
Etal
Mellerstain House
Sweethope Hill
Stichill
Birgham
Carham
Wark
East Learmouth
Crookham
Branxton
Ford
Earlston
Redpath
Smailholm
Nenthorn
Ednam
West Learmouth
Pressen
Flodden
Smailholm Tower
Hendersyde Park
Hadden
Sprouston
Floors Castle
Abbey
KELSO
Maxwellheugh
Downham
Howtel
Milfield
Kimmer
Fenton
Bemersyde
Makerstoun
Lempitlaw
Mindrum
Pawston
Kilham
Housedon Hill
Clintmains
Dryburgh Abbey
St Boswells
Trows
Roxburgh
Heiton
Blakelaw
Hoselaw Loch
Shotton
Westnewton
Lanton
Coupland
R Glen
Kirknewton
Yeavering Bell
Akeld
Humbleton
Rutherford
Maxton
Bowmont Forest
Linton Hill
Town Yetholm
Kirk Yetholm
Coldsmouth Hill
Hethpool
Newton Tors
DERE STREET
Fairnington
Peniel Heugh
Crookhouse
Linton
Kale Water
Whitelaw
Fredden Hill
Earle
Middleton Hall
Belses
Ancrum
Nisbet
Eckford
Morebattle
Crookedshaws Hill
Steer Rig
North Middleton
Crailing
Castle Cessford
Hownam Law
The Curr
The Schil
Preston Hill
Cold Law
Langlee Crags
Chesters
Lanton
Crailinghall
Whitton
Fort
Mowhaugh
Sourhope
THE CHEVIOT
Langleeford
JEDBURGH
Newton
Abbey
Howgate
Auchope Cairn
Hedgehope Hill
Hundalee
Dunion Hill
Bedrule
Hownam
Craik Moor
Comb Fell
Dunmoor Hill
Ferniehirst Castle
Oxnam
Chatto
Swinside Hall
Cock Law
Linhope
Hartside
Bairnkine
Mossburnford
Whitestone Hill
Mozie Law
Windy Gyle
Shill Moor
Bloodybush Edge
Beefstand
Falla
Mervinslaw
Camptown
ROMAN CAMPS
Loft
Cushat Law
High Knowes
Abbotrule
Woden Law
Nether Hindhope
Blindburn
Bell Hill
Barrowburn
Wether Cairn
Cleuch Head
Chesters
Hass
Pienderleith
Philip Law
Upper Hindhope
Leithope Forest
Grindstone Law
Southdean
Huntford
Deerlee Knowe
ROMAN
Biddlestone
Shillmoor
L A M M E R M U I R H I L L S
M E R S E
C H E V I O T H I L L S

Keymap 2

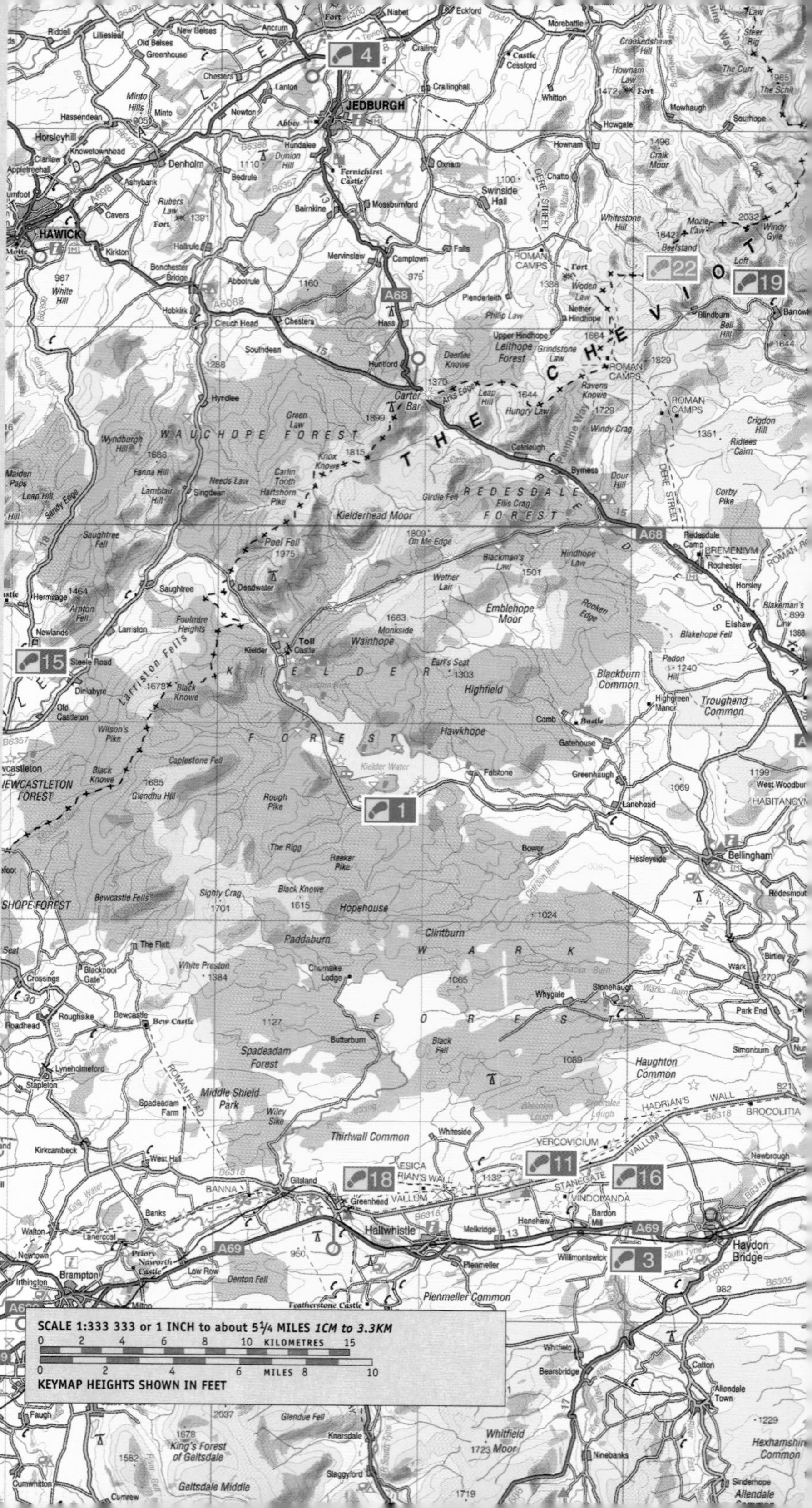

SCALE 1:333 333 or 1 INCH to about 5¼ MILES 1CM to 3.3KM
0 2 4 6 8 10 KILOMETRES 15
0 2 4 6 MILES 8 10
KEYMAP HEIGHTS SHOWN IN FEET
JEDBURGH
HAWICK
THE CHEVIOTS
WAUCHOPE FOREST
REDESDALE FOREST
KIELDER FOREST
WARK FOREST
NEWCASTLETON FOREST
Carter Bar
Peel Fell
Kielder Water
Bellingham
Haltwhistle
Haydon Bridge
Brampton
HADRIAN'S WALL
VERCOVICIUM
VINDOLANDA
BREMENIVM
HABITANCVM
BROCOLITIA
Spadeadam Forest
Thirlwall Common
Kielderhead Moor
Emblehope Moor
Larriston Fells
DERE STREET
ROMAN CAMPS
Pennine Way
A68
A69
4
22
19
15
1
18
11
16
3

THE CHEVIOT
Alnwick
Alnmouth
Warkworth
Rothbury
Harwood Forest
Otterburn
Morpeth
Ashington
Bedlington
Ponteland
Newcastle upon Tyne
Wallsend
Gateshead
Hexham
Corbridge
Prudhoe
Blaydon
Whickham
Stanley
Consett
Chester
Longbenton
Slaley Forest
Blanchland
Belsay
Elsdon
Cambo
Wallington
Kirkwhelpington
Ridsdale
Rothley
Longhorsley
Felton
Widdrington
Longhoughton
Craster
Embleton
Dunstanburgh Castle
Thrunton Wood
Edlingham
Whittingham
Powburn
Ingram
Alwinton
Harbottle
Holystone
Sharperton
Ryton
Painshawfield
Riding Mill
Chopwell
Burnopfield
Rowlands Gill
Wylam
Throckley
Darras Hall
Pegswood
Stannington
Kirkharle
Capheaton
Matfen
Stamfordham
Humshaugh
Chollerton
Barrasford
Acomb
Newton
Stocksfield
Ovingham
Ovington
Horsley
Heddon-on-the-Wall
Dere Street
Devil's Causeway
Roman Road
Hadrian's Wall
A1
A68
A69
A696
A697
A1068
A692
A693
A184
A194(M)

At-a-glance...

Walk	Page	Start	Nat. Grid Reference	Distance	Time	Highest Point
Above Rothbury	40	Rothbury	NU 050015	5 miles (8km)	3 hrs	787ft (240m)
Allen Banks	18	Allen Banks, near Bardon Mill	NY 797640	3 miles (4.8km)	1½ hrs	492ft (150m)
Arnton Fell	46	Between Newlands and Steele Rd	NY 514932	5½ miles (8.9km)	3 hrs	1378ft (420m)
Around the Cheviot from Harthope valley	86	Harthope valley	NT 955226	12 miles (19.3km)	6½ hrs	2526ft (770m)
Blanchland	16	Blanchland	NY 965504	3½ miles (5.6km)	2 hrs	1165ft (355m)
Cauldshiels Loch and the River Tweed	61	Gun Knowe Loch, Galashiels	NT 517345	9½ miles (15.3km)	4 hrs	951ft (290m)
Coldingham Bay and St Abb's Head	30	Coldingham	NT 915665	6½ miles (10.5km)	3½ hrs	262ft (80m)
Craster and Dunstanburgh Castle	26	Craster	NU 256198	4½ miles (7.2km)	2½ hrs	131ft (40m)
Craster, Howick and Longhoughton	80	Craster	NU 256198	8 miles (12.9km)	4 hrs	164ft (50m)
Doddington Moor	22	Doddington	NU 000324	4 miles (6.4km)	2 hrs	600ft (183m)
Eccles Cairn and the College valley	70	Hethpool	NT 893285	7½ miles (12.1km)	3½ hrs	1181ft (360m)
Grey Mare's Tail and Loch Skeen	64	Grey Mare's Tail NTS car park	NT 186145	6½ miles (10.5km)	4½ hrs	2493ft (760m)
Hadrian's Wall at Walltown and Thirlwall Castle	55	Walltown	NY 675662	7½ miles (12.1km)	4 hrs	935ft (285m)
Hadrian's Wall from Steel Rigg	34	Steel Rigg	NY 750676	5 miles (8km)	2½ hrs	1066ft (325m)
Hadrian's Wall: Vindolanda and Housesteads	48	Housesteads Fort	NY 793683	7 miles (11.3km)	4½ hrs	1066ft (325m)
Hartside, Salter's Road and High Cantle	73	Hartside	NT 975161	8 miles (12.9km)	4½ hrs	1542ft (470m)
Kelso, Roxburgh and the River Teviot	37	Kelso	NT 727339	8 miles (12.9km)	4 hrs	164ft (50m)
Kielder Water – the Bull Crag peninsula	14	Bull Crag	NY 675866	3 miles (4.8km)	1½ hrs	656ft (200m)
Kirk Yetholm and the Halterburn valley	77	Kirk Yetholm	NT 827281	8 miles (12.9km)	4½ hrs	1575ft (480m)
Melrose and the Eildon Hills	52	Melrose	NT 547339	5½ miles (8.9km)	3 hrs	1385ft (422m)
Peebles and the River Tweed	43	Peebles	NT 250403	7½ miles (12.1km)	3½ hrs	607ft (185m)
Peniel Heugh	20	Harestanes Visitor Centre, nr Ancrum	NT 641244	3½ miles (5.6km)	2 hrs	774ft (237m)
St Mary's Loch	28	St Mary's Loch	NT 238204	7½ miles (12.1km)	3½ hrs	984ft (300m)
Simonside	24	Simonside Forest Park	NZ 036996	4 miles (6.4km)	2½ hrs	1409ft (430m)
Traquair and Minch Moor	83	Traquair Centre, nr Ancrum	NT 330346	10 miles (16.1km)	5 hrs	1860ft (567m)
Whiteadder valley and Edin's Hall Broch	32	Abbey St Bathans	NT 762619	5 miles (8km)	2½ hrs	722ft (220m)
Windy Gyle	58	Near Windyhaugh, nr Alwinton	NT 859114	7 miles (11.3km)	4½ hrs	2031ft (619m)
Yearning Saddle and Deel's Hill	67	Blindburn Bridge	NT 830109	7½ miles (12.1km)	4 hrs	1624ft (495m)

Comments

There is an energetic start to this walk as it climbs out of Rothbury up to the woods and moorland overlooking the town. After this the going is easier and the views are magnificent.

Allen Banks is a beauty spot on the River Allen cared for by the National Trust, who maintain footpaths that extend to the tarn in Morralee Wood, which can be seen if you make a detour.

On this remote moorland walk close to Hermitage Castle, there are grand views looking down Liddlesdale.

This is a demanding route for experienced walkers with a compass. Be sure of a good forecast – although the gradients are comparatively easy, a strong wind can be an energy-sapping adversary.

Blanchland is one of England's most beautiful villages as well as being one of the most remote. The walker will climb to open moorland before returning along the unspoilt bank of the River Derwent.

This route provides a good day's walking in the pastoral countryside south of Galashiels. The return uses the riverside path on the west bank of the Tweed.

A superb coast walk that takes you from a sandy bay through an attractive fishing village and around a spectacular headland. There is also a pleasant inland return route.

The clifftop path northwards from Craster to Dunstanburgh makes an ever-popular stroll but beyond the castle the route will become less crowded, and the last part follows a volcanic sill.

The coastline to the south of Craster is much less frequented than the popular stretch northwards to Dunstanburgh. However, it holds many delights, which can be fine seashore picnic places.

This gentle walk takes you onto the open moorland that overlooks the village of Doddington. A glance at the map shows this was a district well favoured by Bronze Age settlers.

This walk provides a good opportunity of appreciating the landscape of the Cheviots. If weather conditions change there are good escape routes off the hill via Trowupburn.

Some steep climbs and rough walking is compensated for by the magnificent views over the Border hills, the wild surroundings of the loch and the dramatic waterfall.

Fewer people walk this stretch of Hadrian's Wall compared with the famous section at Highshield Crags. The latter part of the route follows the *vallum*, the defensive ditch on the south side of the wall.

This is one of Britain's classic walks with its outstanding views of Hadrian's Wall snaking across a highland wilderness. On fine days in high summer it is advisable to start early to avoid the crowds.

The walk links the two best-preserved and most interesting Roman forts and includes the most dramatic stretch of Hadrian's Wall.

It is as well to take a compass with you on this excursion into the Cheviots. For three-quarters of the route no habitation is visible and for half the distance the paths are little more than sheep-tracks.

A particularly attractive walk along the banks of the River Teviot takes you from Kelso to the village of Roxburgh.

Kielder Water is the largest man-made lake in Europe, and this short and easy route is an excellent way of appreciating its character, the path following the shoreline of a small peninsula.

There is plenty of climbing – long and steady rather than steep – on this walk in the Cheviots, parts of which are right on the border between Scotland and England.

A steep climb to the summit of the Eildons, with magnificent viewpoints, is followed by a descent to the banks of the Tweed and a relaxing return to Melrose.

The walk goes through a particularly attractive stretch of the Tweed valley, passing the splendidly sited Neidpath Castle just to the west of Peebles.

From the wooded surroundings of the Harestanes Visitor Centre, the route heads up to a fine viewpoint monument overlooking the Teviot valley.

This easy circuit of St Mary's Loch, the largest expanse of water in the Borders, provides a succession of outstanding views.

This route is clearly waymarked by the Forestry Commission, and those following it will enjoy the succession of views along the ridge of the Simonside Hills, overlooking much of Northumbria.

A steady climb along a clear track up to the magnificent viewpoint of Minch Moor is followed by a descent through conifers and a walk just above the River Tweed.

From the lonely and atmospheric remains of Edin's Hall Broch, there are fine views over the valley of Whiteadder Water towards the Lammermuirs.

There is a short episode of energetic climbing to the Cheviot ridge, but after this the walking is undemanding though you should not begin this expedition unless conditions are good.

Be prepared for wet feet up to the ridge of the Cheviots and the Pennine Way. The landscape here is bleak and beautiful, and the peace is undisturbed (unless the army are at gunnery practice!).

Introduction to Northumberland, the Borders and Hadrian's Wall

The peace and tranquillity of the rolling and thinly populated countryside on both sides of the English-Scottish border is something of a deception, largely disguising the fact that for centuries this was the most violent and bloodstained piece of land in Britain. However, a closer look at the landscape reveals not only medieval castles and walled towns but also peel towers, or mini-castles, that protected manors and individual farmhouses.

Most impressive of this array of fortifications is the earliest, the Roman wall built by Emperor Hadrian.

Hadrian's Wall

Although no longer on the line of the border between England and Scotland, Hadrian's Wall represents the first attempt to define the boundary between the northern and southern halves of the island of Britain. Constructed on the orders of Emperor Hadrian around AD122, it snakes across the country from the Solway Firth in the west to the mouth of the Tyne in the east, a distance of 73 miles (117km). It marked the northern limits of the Roman advance – at least for the time being – and created a specific frontier between Roman Britain to the south and the unsubdued tribes of Caledonia to the north.

Hadrian's Wall was just one part – albeit the most important – of what was a huge and elaborate military complex. Along its length were 17 forts and, at intervals of approximately 1 mile (1.6km), mini-forts or milecastles were constructed to provide extra defence. On the north side there was a V-shaped ditch, except where the wall runs along the top of steep cliffs, and to the south a broad, flat-bottomed ditch called the vallum. In addition there were a number of supply bases and auxiliary forts to the south of the wall which pre-dated both the wall and its forts. There were designated crossing-points, mostly at the forts and milecastles, where both people and trade could pass through. Despite being such a complex defence system, Hadrian's Wall was breached several times and temporarily abandoned when the Romans pushed their frontier further north to the Clyde-Forth valley. It fell into disuse and was finally abandoned towards the end of the 4th century, when Roman power in Britain was on the verge of collapse.

Although mostly destroyed at both its western and eastern ends – in the east the wall is covered by the suburbs of Newcastle and the adjoining towns – substantial portions remain in the more thinly populated middle stretches. The unique historical appeal and significance of Hadrian's Wall, a World Heritage site, coupled with the ruggedly beautiful landscape through which it passes, gives it a unique atmosphere. Both the wall and the area around it make marvellous walking country and the line of the wall is currently being developed as a new National Trail.

Borders

Running like a silvan thread through the heart of the Borders is the River Tweed, famed both for its natural beauty and its salmon-fishing. Many of the Border towns are situated either near its banks or those of its many tributaries. To the south and west of the Tweed valley rises the Tweedsmuir range, which contains some of the

loneliest, wildest and most sparsely populated country in the Borders. Here is also where the highest summit is to be found, Broad Law (2756ft/840m). The hills surrounding the valleys of the Yarrow and Ettrick to the west of Selkirk once formed part of Ettrick Forest, a hunting-ground for medieval Scottish kings. Now they are a forest in the modern sense, with many of the slopes covered with conifer plantations.

The harbour at St Abbs

To the north and east of the Tweed, the Moorfoot and Lammermuir hills stretch towards the North Sea coast. These are lower and have more gentle gradients but are noted for their excellent walking and magnificent views that can extend right across southern Scotland from Edinburgh to the English border. Almost enclosed in a horseshoe between these hills and the Cheviots is the rich farming country of the Merse, the coastal lowlands of Berwickshire.

Sir Walter Scott, the most famous son of the Borders, loved this area, and a visit to his favourite viewpoint on Bemersyde Hill, near Melrose, will illustrate why. In front of you the distinctive triple-peaked Eildon Hills rise above the surrounding low-lying country while below you the Tweed makes a great loop around their base; arguably the finest view in the whole of southern Scotland.

Northumberland

Covering an area of 396 sq miles (1026 sq km), the Northumberland National Park is one of Britain's smaller national parks. It comprises the most spectacular part of Hadrian's Wall and from there extends northwards through part of the Border forests, through wooded river valleys and over the heather-covered sandstone Simonside Hills to the Cheviots, the northernmost part of the Pennine range. Much of the Cheviots comprises remote and lonely country with relatively few out-standing landmarks, and walkers are warned not to venture onto the hills in bad weather, especially misty conditions, unless experienced in both map- and compass-reading.

There is far more to Northumberland than the area covered by the National Park. A number of rivers rise on the slopes of the Cheviots – Aln, Coquet and North Tyne – and make their way through lovely valleys and past quiet towns and villages to the coastal lowlands and the North Sea. The coast is one of the jewels of the county, with a succession of magnificent sandy beaches and a string of dramatically sited castles stretching southwards from Berwick-Upon-Tweed towards the Tyne. Bamburgh and Dunstanburgh are the most striking of these coastal castles but there are two others just inland – Warkworth, which has a commanding position above the River Coquet, and Alnwick, for centuries the seat of the dukes of Northumberland.

Parts of the coastline are protected by the National Trust, including the stretches on both sides of Dunstanburgh Castle. The Trust also has extensive interests elsewhere in the region, owning stately properties such as Lindisfarne Castle, Wallington Hall and the fascinating Victorian mansion and estate at Cragside. It also has what is probably the most dramatic stretch of Hadrian's Wall, 4$^{1}/_{2}$ miles (7.2km) near the fort at Housesteads.

Rivalling Hadrian's Wall both in historic interest and atmosphere is Holy Island or Lindisfarne, reached from the mainland by a causeway and cut off for part of the day. Here is where the Celtic missionary St Aidan first brought Christianity to Northumbria and founded a monastery in the 7th century. The island possesses the rich red sandstone ruins of a Norman priory and a restored 16th-century castle, the latter built to protect the island from Scottish raids.

To the west of the National Park is Kielder Water, the largest man-made lake in Europe, surrounded by the plantations of Kielder Forest, part of the vast Border forests. Here there are numerous car parks and picnic sites and miles of footpaths and cycle trails to enable visitors to enjoy the great outdoors.

History
Throughout the Middle Ages and after, repeated attempts by English kings to conquer Scotland, spirited Scottish resistance and counter-invasions, Scotland's alliance with England's traditional enemy France, and constant raids by ruthless and lawless barons from both sides of the border led to almost constant warfare. Only with the union of the two crowns under James VI of Scotland and I of England in 1603, followed by the Act of Union between the two countries a century later, did peace finally come to the region.

Nowhere illustrates this troubled history more than the town of Berwick-Upon-Tweed. During its long history it has changed hands between the two kingdoms no less than thirteen times, until becoming permanently part of England in 1482.

Walking in the area
With a mixture of empty rolling hills and expansive moorlands, pleasant river valleys, extensive forests, fertile lowlands and an impressive coastline, there is plenty of superb and varied walking country on both sides of the border. Although lacking the craggy majesty of the Scottish Highlands or the mountains of Snowdonia and the English Lake District, the Border hills offer plenty of

Craster harbour

challenging walks and, like all upland regions, should be treated with caution and respect and never be underestimated, especially in bad weather. On many of the routes you can walk for hours on most days without meeting a soul.

Although most walkers will inevitably make for the hills, the coast and lowlands also have their attractions. There are many fine, bracing walks along the cliffs and beaches of both the Berwickshire and Northumberland coasts, and delightful walks can be enjoyed in the valleys of the Tweed, Teviot, Aln, Coquet and the North and South Tyne. On both sides of the border, the well-waymarked trails in the Forestry Commission plantations make for attractive and generally trouble-free walking and there are a number of lochs and reservoirs, large and small, throughout the region. Walking is further enhanced by the wealth of historic monuments. Foremost among these are the quartet of Scottish Border abbeys – Kelso, Melrose, Dryburgh and Jedburgh – the castles of the Northumberland coast, Lindisfarne Priory on Holy Island, and of course Hadrian's Wall.

Three National Trails cross the region. One – currently in the process of being completed – follows the line of Hadrian's Wall from coast to coast. The final part of the Pennine Way – at least for walkers starting from its southern end – coincides with the Hadrian's Wall Path for a short distance and then turns northwards and continues through part of the Border forests and across the Cheviots to end just over the Scottish border at Kirk Yetholm. The cross-country Southern Upland Way winds its way across the empty hills of the Scottish Borders to reach the Berwick-shire coast at Cockburnspath.

St Cuthbert's Way is a recently created long-distance route that runs for approximately 62 miles (100km) from Melrose to Lindisfarne, physically linking Scotland and England and tracing the footsteps of one of the early saints who spread Christianity throughout this part of Britain. On the way it passes through a still wild, beautiful and largely unspoilt landscape, parts of which can have changed little since the saint himself journeyed this way.

Northumberland National Park is one of the most beautiful areas of England. At its core, the hills and moors are open and apparently empty. They give a glimpse of wilderness and solitude, a sense of harmony with nature which is rare and precious in our crowded island. This is 'the land of the far horizon'.

That people have touched this land lightly is, to an extent, an illusion. Tides of history, the hopes and dreams of empires and kings, have ebbed and flowed across these Borderlands. So have the lives of shepherds and labourers.

Few places in England can boast such a rich archaeological record, spanning more than 7,000 years of occupation. This is also frontier territory in which the Hadrian's Wall complex and the bastle and peel towers from the turbulent Anglo-Scottish wars represents a unique built heritage.

The sense of continuity is also important. These are living landscapes with a community, still largely dependent on farming, with whom we must work and whose interests, activities and traditions we must respect.

Our essential vision for the future of the National Park is of a partnership with the community of the Park to conserve its characteristic beauty and the natural and man-made heritage, both for its own sake and in order that it may continue to be a source of refreshment, inspiration and delight to those who visit it.

Graham Taylor, Chief Executive
Northumberland National Park Authority

Kielder Water – the Bull Crag peninsula

Start	Bull Crag (the promontory due west of Tower Knowe Information Centre, Kielder Water)
Distance	3 miles (4.8km)
Approximate time	1½ hours
Parking	Bull Crag
Refreshments	None
Ordnance Survey maps	Landranger 80 (Cheviot Hills & Kielder Forest), Explorer OL42 (Kielder Water & Forest - Bellingham & Simonside Hills)

This is a short and undemanding walk that allows the visitor to appreciate the beauty of Kielder Water as well as its vast scale. The largest man-made lake in Europe, it covers 2684 acres (1086 ha), is 9 miles (14.5km) long and contains 41,350m gallons (188,000m litres) of water. The scheme began in 1976 and was completed six years later. In summer a waterbus service allows visitors to explore remote shores out of the reach of roads. The route does not dwell overlong amongst pine trees and is well waymarked in the usual Forestry Commission manner.

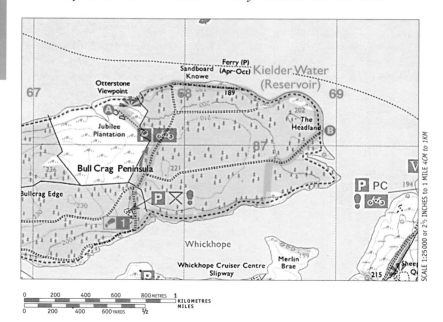

Kielder Water from the Otterstone viewpoint

There are orange waymarks to lead you round this route from the car park and picnic site at Bull Crag (there are toilets here too).

Start by returning up the track that has brought you to the car park and turn right at the top, following a sign to the Otterstone viewpoint. The road forks on two occasions; bear left each time to reach the car park at Otterstone. The viewpoint **Ⓐ**, which certainly provides a splendid vista of lake and forest, is set amongst a lovely group of ancient Scots pines. From here it is easy to appreciate that this is the largest forest in Britain, covering about 200 sq miles (518 sq km). There were few trees in this vast area of moorland when planting began in 1926.

The path doglegs down to the shore, crossing a fence to head eastwards (for a short stretch through trees where evil-looking redcap toadstools show themselves in autumn). After this the path joins a section of the old main road that once ran through the valley of the North Tyne. Most of it was covered by water many years ago, and in fact this portion too vanishes below the waters of the reservoir. However, our way is to the right, continuing along the shore towards the Headland. There is a good view of the dam from here as the path threads through heather. The dam measures ¾ mile (1.2km) long and 169ft (52m) high.

Having skirted the Headland, the path leaves the waterside **Ⓑ** to head into the forest. If you are fortunate you may catch a glimpse of a great spotted woodpecker or even a crossbill amongst the trees here. The latter's crossed mandibles allow it to extract pine seeds from tightly closed cones. Also coal-tits and redpolls flourish in pine forests. A large, cleared area on the left allows a glimpse of the reservoir. At the end of the felled section the way bears left to dive into a short, gloomy stretch through the trees. This emerges into a firebreak which is rather boggy. The busy Whickhope Marina can be seen below. The path twists through the mature pines that overlook this creek, soon reaching the starting point at the Bull Crag picnic site again. ●

Blanchland

Start	Blanchland
Distance	3½ miles (5.6km)
Approximate time	2 hours
Parking	Blanchland
Refreshments	Pub and café at Blanchland
Ordnance Survey maps	Landranger 87 (Hexham & Haltwhistle), Explorer OL43 (Hadrian's Wall-Haltwhistle & Hexham)

Blanchland is justly famous as one of England's most beautiful villages. Situated in the wooded valley of the River Derwent (which here forms the boundary between Northumberland and County Durham), its honey-coloured houses, made from the fabric of the monastery, huddle around the ancient abbey church. The moors rise up on all sides. Its famous hotel, the Lord Crewe Arms, was once the guesthouse of the abbey and provides refreshments for walkers in the bar. Look out for its ghosts! The short walk takes you up to the open moorland and then drops to the Derwent for a riverbank walk back to Blanchland.

Turn left out of the car park and climb the lane through woodland. From April until July the verges and hedgerows are ablaze with a glorious variety of wild flowers. The lane is made up as far as Shildon, where on the left you can see the remains of old lead-mine workings. Above Shildon the lane becomes a farm track but the walking is still comfortable. Look for northern marsh orchids in the ditch on the right as the track emerges into more open country.

Pennypie House appears ahead. This farm apparently got its name from the pies it baked and sold for a penny to the miners who used the track to get to their work. Pass through a gate on to the open moor **Ⓐ** but resist the temptation to continue to climb further on this track. Instead, turn to the left at the gate onto another track, which runs

Blanchland

SCALE 1:25 000 or 2½ INCHES to 1 MILE 4CM to 1KM

duckboarding takes the path to the riverbank, and it then runs close by the river through woodland and meadows to Blanchland. It is easy to linger on this part of the walk, especially on a warm day. There is nothing more soothing than the sound of rushing water and sunlight highlighting its passage through a canopy of overhanging trees.

At the bridge at Blanchland turn left to walk through the village to the car park, passing the Lord Crewe Arms, the medieval gatehouse and the abbey church on the way. Most of the fabric of the abbey was incorporated into the village buildings when Blanchland was rebuilt as a model village in the mid-18th century. Only the chancel of the abbey church was saved and this was adopted as the parish church. It was restored again in Victorian times. Interesting coffin lids are to be seen in the floor of the transept: two depict abbots who hold their pastoral staff, while the third shows the huntsman to the abbey, Robert de Egylston, with the tools of his trade – a horn, arrow and sword.

A red-haired monk is one of two ghosts that haunt the Lord Crewe Arms. The other is the shade of Dorothy Forster, who helped her brother Tom, a Jacobite general, to evade pursuers by concealing him in a priest hole. Earlier she had helped him escape from Newgate Prison. Her ghost appears to implore visitors to take a message to him in France, where he eventually took refuge.

southwards with the wall on the left. The views from here over the village to the moorland on the other side of the Derwent valley are magical and the going easy on a grassy path. Lapwings and curlews nest in the tussocky moorland here; the latter, with its curved beak and spine-tingling, unearthly call, is the symbol of the Northumberland National Park.

A gas-line pumping station on the right heralds the end of this too-brief moorland interlude. Follow the metalled lane downhill from this point **B**: it descends steeply to the road at Baybridge but there are still impressive panoramas to enjoy *en route*.

At the road, turn right and walk past the Carricks picnic site to the bridge. Turn left **C** just before the bridge onto the footpath that follows the north bank of the Derwent. A causeway of

Allen Banks

Start	Allen Banks, near Bardon Mill
Distance	3 miles (4.8km)
Approximate time	1½ hours
Parking	National Trust car park and picnic site at Allen Banks
Refreshments	None
Ordnance Survey maps	Landrangers 86 (Haltwhistle, Bewcastle & Alston) and 87 (Hexham & Haltwhistle), Explorer OL43 (Hadrian's Wall-Haltwhistle & Hexham)

The National Trust have done a wonderful job in opening up the footpaths in and around the 200 acres (81 ha) of Allen Banks. In its own way this property is almost as spectacular as Cragside, the River Allen having cut a precipitous gorge here on its course to join the Tyne. Fine trees grow by the river and on the steep sides of its valley, making excellent habitats for many birds, including woodpeckers. Allen Banks is also one of the last refuges of the red squirrel in this country, though you will be fortunate indeed if you see one. An extra 1½-mile (2.4km) excursion can be made to the tarn in Morralee Wood; it is Northumberland's answer to Tarn Hows – a really idyllic spot. Dogs are not allowed on part of the route.

The National Trust's car park was once the walled garden of Ridley Hall, seat of one of the most celebrated of Northumbrian families. Take the riverside path and after ½ mile (800m) – before the bridge – look for steps on the right that lead to a steep path climbing to the top of the steep-sided valley. A stile here gives access into Ridley Park (you can just see the house). Do not cross this but turn left Ⓐ onto the path that runs along the side of the park fence.

The path still climbs, though not so severely, as it passes fine specimens of beech and oak. The River Allen is now far below. Sheep graze on the other side of the fence, and there is a super-abundance of pheasants here.

For a while there are trees to both sides of the path but eventually the fence returns on the right. When the way ahead is stopped by a steep ravine, look for the Bone-floor Viewpoint, a circular clearing of about 10ft (3m) diameter, floored with the knuckle-bones of sheep. It is well camouflaged by a growth of moss. Take the steep, zigzag path down here by the side of the stream and be especially careful if the steps are wet or covered with leaves. Turn right onto the riverside path, crossing the footbridge Ⓑ.

The path winds beneath magnificent, tall pines. A diversion can be made to the right, through Briarwood Bank Nature Reserve, which is owned by the Northumberland Wildlife Trust.

However, please note that dogs are not allowed here.

Cross the footbridge over the small stream and continue along the riverside path to the suspension bridge **C**, which provides an exciting way over the Allen. On the eastern bank take the lane from Plankey Mill, which climbs steeply, and then the track that forks off to the left. After 50 yds (46m) a stile leads to the riverside footpath, which passes through a meadow and then runs alongside a beautifully rebuilt stone wall. After a pastoral interlude the path comes again to the gorge. Keep to the lower path, which zigzags around enormous boulders that have fallen from above. Steps lead to a high path above the crags, which looks adventurous.

Our way close to the rushing waters of the lovely river should not be hurried. Herons will flap lazily from their favourite fishing-haunts. Dippers hop from rock to rock, and occasionally you may see or hear a large salmon leap at a fly – this stretch of river is a sanctuary for fish. In places the path is being undermined, so take great care when it becomes narrow approaching the bridge. This route does not require the bridge **D** to be crossed (if the planks are wet this can demand steady nerves).

If you wish to make a 1½-mile (2.4km) detour to visit Morralee Wood and the enchanting tarn within it, take the route marked with white-painted tops (the route back from the tarn is not marked). Take the steps to the right and then turn right again, following the posts and, on two occasions, a rock engraved 'To Tarn'. Keep climbing steps to cross the upper path mentioned earlier and keep straight on as the view opens up over the Tyne valley. After more pleasant walking the path does a U-turn and climbs steeply through tall pines to reach the attractive tarn. Keep on the path to the right of the tarn, and

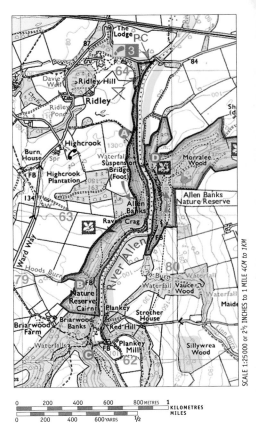

spare a moment to enjoy the view: Ridley Hall can be seen through the trees. The way back owes much to instinct. There is a maze of paths here but no white posts as guides. The main path climbs steeply from the tarn. Take this and keep straight on through avenues of rhododendrons to reach a path running along the side of the valley. At first this seems as though it may lead you back to Plankey Mill, but eventually it plunges down to a lower path that follows the river back to the bridge at **D**.

From here the path along the eastern bank of the River Allen runs through field and meadow to reach the road bridge. Pass beneath this to find the gate onto the road and then cross the bridge to reach the starting point at the car park. ●

Peniel Heugh

Start	Harestanes Visitor Centre, 1 mile (1.6km) east of Ancrum
Distance	3½ miles (5.6km)
Approximate time	2 hours
Parking	Harestanes Visitor Centre
Refreshments	Tearoom at the visitor centre (open April–October)
Ordnance Survey maps	Landranger 74 (Kelso), Explorer OL16 (The Cheviot Hills)

This well-waymarked route starts at the Harestanes Visitor Centre, converted from a former sawmill and open from the beginning of April to the end of October. It climbs steadily through woodland to reach the summit of Peniel Heugh at 774ft (237m), a magnificent viewpoint crowned by the Waterloo Monument. On both the ascent and descent, gaps in the trees reveal grand views across the Border country to the Cheviots, and there is much fine woodland near the start and finish of the walk.

Turn right out of the car park along a tarmac drive, shortly continuing along an enclosed path parallel to the drive. Follow this path as it turns right Ⓐ to continue through woodland – a most attractive route with some fine ancient trees lining the path.

The Waterloo Monument on Peniel Heugh

At a finger-post, turn right to cross a footbridge over a burn and turn left at another finger-post Ⓑ to continue along a tree-lined path to reach the tarmac drive to Monteviot House, seat of the marquesses of Lothian, to the right. Turn left along the drive to a road, cross over and continue along the drive opposite. At a fork in front of a house, continue along the right-hand track and, about 50 yds (46m) further on, turn right onto a track that winds along the right edge of woodland, ascending steadily and bearing left into the trees to reach a lane Ⓒ.

Turn right and almost immediately turn left to continue quite steeply uphill through trees. Gaps in the trees on the right reveal superb views over the Teviot valley to the Cheviots beyond. At a fork, continue along the left-hand track and at the next fork continue again along the left-hand track. On nearing the edge of the woodland, the Waterloo Monument can be seen straight ahead.

A few yards before emerging from the trees, bear left along a track that continues uphill through woodland, curving right to reach a kissing-gate. Go through, turn left, continue uphill by a wall on the left and, where the wall bends left, keep straight ahead to reach the monument **D**. This is a magnificent all-round viewpoint, with the winding Teviot below and the Eildons and Cheviots standing out prominently. The

150ft- (46m) high monument was erected by the 6th Marquess of Lothian to commemorate the Duke of Wellington's victory at the Battle of Waterloo and was started soon after the battle was fought in 1815. Around it are the remains of some of the earthworks of two forts: one Iron Age and one from the Dark Ages.

Retrace your steps to descend through the woods as far as the first finger-post **B**. Here do not follow the outward route to the right but keep ahead, in the direction of the 'visitor centre', along another attractive tree-lined track. Look out for where way-marks direct you to the right off the track to continue along a path by a burn on the right. Cross a footbridge over the burn, continue to a tarmac track and turn right along it to return to the start. ●

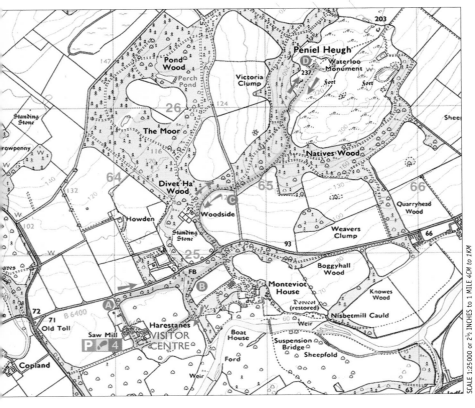

Doddington Moor

Start	Doddington
Distance	4 miles (6.4km)
Approximate time	2 hours
Parking	Layby at Doddington village cross or off-road in lane opposite
Refreshments	None
Ordnance Survey maps	Landranger 75 (Berwick-upon-Tweed), Explorers 339 (Kelso, Coldstream & Lower Tweed Valley) and 340 (Holy Island & Bamburgh)

It is not difficult to see why Doddington Moor was popular with prehistoric Northumbrians. Although breezy, its wide horizons gave plenty of warning of enemies approaching. It makes a good walk – a gentle ascent on a firm track is followed by stretches across pasture and heather. Although the moor is littered with prehistoric monuments, only the larger ones are obvious on the ground.

Take the lane up from the stone cross towards Wooler Golf Club. As for so much of this walk, there are fine views of the Cheviots, though on the way up the hill you have to pause and turn to appreciate them.

The lane goes off to the right to the golf club, but our way lies ahead through the gate onto a sandy track that continues to climb. However, it dips briefly by sheep-pens where a shepherd's mobile home stands close by.

New plantations have been established on the left, which in later years will screen the views in this direction. As the track levels out, look for a gate on the right Ⓐ with a sign to Weetwood Hill and take this path across a large pasture. Head to the left of the clump of trees on the skyline and, when you meet the wall at the top, turn right to reach this spinney, called Kitty's Plantation. At this point Ⓑ you may look back to see the most obvious of Doddington's

Bronze Age monuments – the fort known as the Ringses. Less obvious are the host of rocks carved with cup-and-ring symbols to be found on the fell-sides around the village. There are said to be more of these within a 5-mile (8km) radius of the village than anywhere else in Britain.

Keep the wall to the left after a gate takes the path onto open moorland. There should be a stone circle at the footpath crossways Ⓒ though it is not apparent on the ground. The path threads its way through high bracken so is easier to distinguish in winter when this has died back. Continue to keep close to the wall. Two lone pines in the field beyond the fence ahead stand as an excellent foreground to a Cheviot panorama.

Turn right at the fence Ⓓ and follow it until the Shepherd's House comes into sight. Make for this on the path up the bracken-covered hillside of Dod Law.

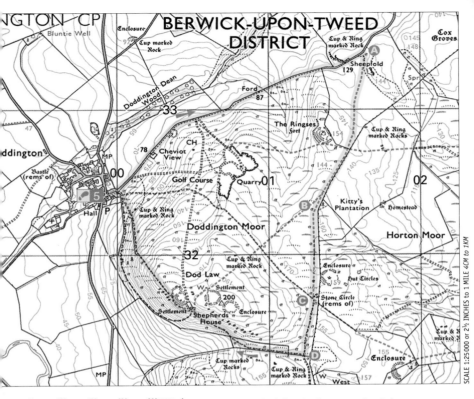

SCALE 1:25 000 or 2½ INCHES to 1 MILE 4CM to 1KM

There are interesting traditions attached to the area just to the south of this hilltop. The Devil is said to have hanged his grandmother over a tall, free-standing block of stone here, which is grooved by the chains he used. Close to this is Cuddy's Cave, used by St Cuthbert when he was a young shepherd. A little further to the south, at the confluence of the rivers Till and Glen, King Arthur fought the first of his twelve great battles.

Walk past the front of the Shepherd's House – it is a landmark from many points in the Cheviots – and continue along the flank of the hill; do not turn right to follow the enclosure wall. There is a thoughtfully sited seat on the right below a golf tee if you care to rest to enjoy the view.

The ruined tower in the farmyard of Doddington Hall below is a 'bastle', which in the Borders is a diminutive of 'castle'. It dates from 1584, a late year for the building of such a stronghold. The path follows a fence and thorn trees down to a stile onto the golf club lane. Turn left, back to the main road. ●

The Shepherd's House on Dod Law

Simonside

Start	Simonside Forest Park, near Rothbury
Distance	4 miles (6.4km)
Approximate time	2½ hours
Parking	Picnic site off the road to Great Tosson, 3 miles (4.8km) south-west of Rothbury off the Hexham road (B6342)
Refreshments	None
Ordnance Survey maps	Landranger 81 (Alnwick & Morpeth), Explorer OL42 (Kielder Water & Forest - Bellingham & Simonside Hills)

The Simonside Hills have a distinctly different appearance to that of the Cheviots. While the latter are gently rounded, these are often likened to a series of choppy breakers. They are darker and more rugged hills than their grander neighbours and from them the views are breathtaking. Altogether, this is one of the Forestry Commission's most enjoyable walks. Although the first part of the route is upwards through the ranks of pines, interest is held by the viewpoints, which occur with regularity. Add to this the usual advantage of having the route impeccably waymarked and you have a perfect recipe for a splendid couple of hours or so.

Before starting, study the map at the picnic site. The one described here is the red route: the Simonside Ridge Walk. All the routes start along the same track, though the easier, green route soon departs. After about twenty minutes steady climbing on a forest track, you come to a seat that overlooks a fine vista of Coquetdale to the Cheviots. The Cheviot is the highest summit to be seen, at 2674ft (815m), with Hedgehope to its right, second-highest at 2343ft (714m). A little further Ⓐ and a short diversion is offered on the left to Little Church Rock. The scramble to the top is rewarding as the tor-like crag is an even better viewpoint than the seat.

Return to the red route, which soon becomes more of a forest path, twisting up through the trees – mainly lodgepole pines – over rough boulders. It emerges on a drive on the open hillside, which in turn you leave when a path makes for the 'dour ridge' of Simonside itself. Rock-climbers enjoy tackling these crags in difficult ways, but the official route is a gentle scramble that results in the capture of the summit Ⓑ at 1409ft (430m), where a cairn offers shelter for the enjoyment of the view: the Cheviots in one direction, the entire stretch of Northumberland's coastline from Tweed to Tyne in the other, and the Coquet, the queen of rivers, can be seen in the near-distance, flowing through the town of Rothbury. Simonside, it is said, is the haunt of mischievous elves known as duegars.

The view from Dove Crag

The path follows the ridge of fell sandstone, its particles of quartz glistening in the light. Grouse whirr away with raucous complaints. Heather-burning takes place on Simonside on a rotational basis as it does throughout the moorland of northern England to provide tender shoots to feed both grouse and sheep.

On the right is Old Stell Crag, whose summit is not climbed. It was the site of the Simonside Beacon, which in the days of the reivers was lit to warn of raids by the Scots. The waymarks lead onto Dove Crag ●, which gives a view of Rothbury and Cragside. The way-marked path descends from the moor after Dove Crag, following alternating sections of broad drives and then narrow paths that wind down steeply through the trees, returning quite suddenly to the picnic site. ●

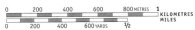

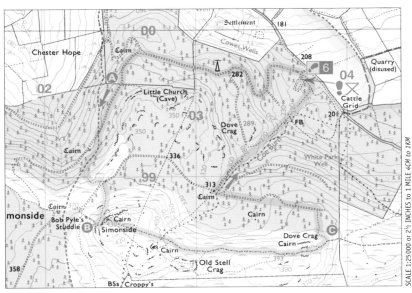

Craster and Dunstanburgh Castle

Start	Craster
Distance	4½ miles (7.2km)
Approximate time	2½ hours
Parking	National Trust car park at Craster
Refreshments	Pubs and seasonal café at Craster
Ordnance Survey maps	Landrangers 75 (Berwick-upon-Tweed) and 81 (Alnwick & Morpeth), Explorer 332 (Alnwick & Amble)

The trouble with really excellent short walks is that they become overcrowded, so choose your time for this one carefully. There are seldom crowds early in the morning when the sea-light on the castle can be magical – as can that of late evening. The drawback to these times is that the opening time for the castle is 10 a.m. and it is closed in the evening.

The National Trust car park at Craster occupies the old quarry, which like most of the village was owned by the family that gave the place its name. The family lived in Craster for more than seven centuries. Whinstone produced by the quarry was sent to London and other great cities where it was used for kerbstones.

A path leads from the quarry to the harbour. Turn northwards from here after taking in the charm of the small fishing village, famous for its delicious oak-smoked kippers. A few picturesque cobles, the distinctive craft of Northumbrian fishermen, usually rest in the harbour; once it was full of them. Craster harbour was built in 1906 by the family as a monument to Captain Craster, who was killed during the British military expedition to Tibet in 1904.

The walk to the castle is on springy turf, with a platform of dolerite on the seaward side providing countless rock pools, which children love to explore, discovering hermit crabs, anemones and periwinkles. This rock is volcanic in origin, intruded between other strata to form the distinctive 'sill' which at its seaward end makes a dramatic, and secure, site for the castle Ⓐ. The path divides at the approach to the castle: take the right fork if you wish to visit it, otherwise take the left through the ditch that once formed the castle's harbour and was used by the fleet of Henry VIII in 1514.

Walking beneath the walls of the stronghold you can appreciate the difficulties faced by those besieging it. Dunstanburgh dates from 1314 and is by far the largest castle in Northumberland, covering 11 acres (4.4 ha). The precipitous dolerite crag forms the perfect defence on the two seaward sides and to the west. Only to the south

The footpath leads northwards beneath the forbidding walls to reach the sea at the south end of Embleton Bay. The seabirds here are mostly kittiwakes, which nest on the rocky ledges of Gull Crag.

There follows a pleasant switchback walk along the crest of the sand-dunes, with a golf course on the left. Note the fantastic swirl of lava on the shore at the beginning of this section, just beyond the gate to Dunstanburgh Stead Links.

The route turns inland on the slatted track **B** that leads to the lane to Dunstan Steads. At the farm, turn left again, following the bridleway sign to Dunstan Square. From the concrete track through fields and meadows there are good views of the castle to the left and of the long sill. Before the concept of landscape conservation took hold, much material was quarried from the sill for roadstone.

On the right is an endless vista of farmland. Trees screen the brickwork of an old lime-kiln that before the advent of artificial fertilizers was vital for cultivation. At Dunstan Square **C** turn left to the Heughs, the local name for the volcanic ridge, then turn right to walk southwards in its shelter, which is welcome when the east wind is blowing. The path is broad at first but becomes narrow after a kissing-gate. It emerges in Craster directly opposite the starting point at car park. ●

does the site lie open, and here the enormous gatehouse with its flanking towers defied attackers. During the Wars of the Roses it was twice besieged by the Earl of Warwick and was surrendered to him on each occasion. Subsequently it was left open to the elements, and these turned it into the picturesque ruin that we see today.

It is hardly surprising that Dunstanburgh has a ghost, a wandering knight named Sir Guy, said to bewail his failure to free a captive maiden, whose ghost appears on the ramparts on wild nights as a white lady.

St Mary's Loch

Start	Southern end of St Mary's Loch
Distance	7½ miles (12.1km)
Approximate time	3½ hours
Parking	Parking-areas at the southern end of the loch and several laybys along the A708
Refreshments	Pub and café at the southern end of the loch
Ordnance Survey maps	Landranger 73 (Peebles, Galashiels & Selkirk), Explorer 337 (Peebles & Innerleithen) and 338 (Galashiels, Selkirk & Melrose)

St Mary's Loch, 3 miles (4.8km) in length, is the largest and, many would argue, the most attractive loch in the Border country. This walk does a circuit of it, using the Southern Upland Way along its eastern shore and mostly following the road along its western shore. The views across the loch's sparkling waters to the encircling steep-sided hills are constantly changing, and the route is both easy to follow and undemanding. The only climb is a short, steep one to the superb viewpoint of St Mary's Kirkyard above the western side of the loch.

Start at the southern end of the loch near the monument to James Hogg (1770–1835), known as the Ettrick Shepherd, and the most famous of the Border poets and a close companion of Sir Walter Scott. Take the road between St Mary's Loch and the adjoining Loch of the Lowes to Tibbie Shiels Inn, a well-known and historic hostelry frequented, among others, by Scott and

At the edge of St Mary's Loch

Hogg. Cross a bridge, turn left at a Southern Upland Way sign to walk through the inn car park and go through a kissing-gate at the far end Ⓐ. Now follow a well-waymarked path along the east side of the loch, over a series of stiles, enjoying the superb views across the water all the while. After passing a farm on the right, join and continue along a farm track below conifers.

Nearing the end of the loch, Dryhope Tower, a peel or fortified tower, can be seen peeping above the trees on the opposite side. Demolished on the orders of James VI at the end of the 16th century, it was later rebuilt but fell into ruin again. Soon after passing the end of the loch, the track curves left Ⓑ to cross a bridge over the River Yarrow and keeps ahead to the road. Turn left and, about 100 yds (91m) after crossing a bridge over a burn, turn right through a gate 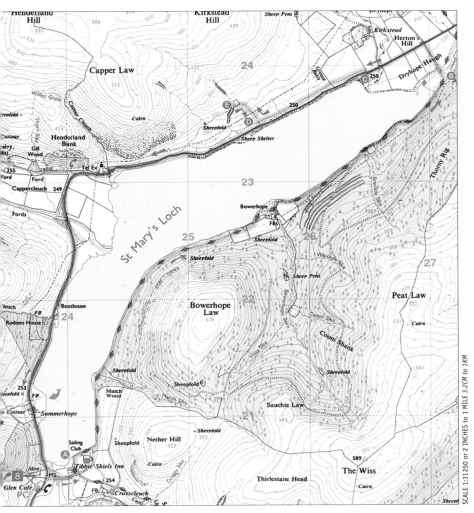, a few yards beyond the wall corner, and turn left along a pleasant, grassy path, parallel to the road and lochside on the left. From this path come more fine views over the loch, and as an alternative you can sometimes walk beside the loch when the water-level is not too high.

Pass through several gates and, when you see a stile and public footpath sign to St Mary's Churchyard below, turn right at a crossing of paths **D** for a brief but worthwhile diversion, following a grassy path steeply uphill and bearing left to reach the churchyard **E**. This place offers possibly the finest view over the loch. The church was destroyed by fire in 1557 and never rebuilt but the churchyard remains.

Retrace your steps downhill, climb the stile onto the road and turn right along it. Follow the road for just over $2\frac{1}{2}$ miles (4km) to return to the start. After a left bend past Clappercleuch, there are good verges and more fine views through trees across the loch. ●

Coldingham Bay and St Abb's Head

Start	Coldingham Bay, ¾ mile (1.2km) east of Coldingham village
Distance	6½ miles (10.5km)
Approximate time	3½ hours
Parking	Coldingham Bay
Refreshments	Beach café (seasonal) at Coldingham Bay, pub at St Abbs, café at Northfield Farm
Ordnance Survey maps	Landranger 67 (Duns, Dunbar & Eyemouth), Explorer 346 (Berwick-upon-Tweed)

There are some spectacular coastal views on this walk, which starts from the sandy curve of Coldingham Bay and continues by way of the fishing village of St Abbs around the sandstone cliffs of St Abb's Head, a nature reserve. As a contrast, the inland return route takes you beside a tree-fringed loch, passes the nature reserve centre and goes through the village of Coldingham with its priory remains, but nowhere are you more than ½ mile (800m) from or out of sight of this glorious rugged coastline.

Start by walking down a tarmac track to the fine beach at Coldingham Bay and turn left along the edge of it. At the far end of the beach, climb steps to the cliff top and turn right to follow a tarmac path for the short distance to St Abbs.

In the village, bear right along a road between single-storey houses and turn right at a T-junction Ⓐ along a road that curves left above the harbour to another T-junction. Turn left, passing to the right of the prominent church, and at a footpath sign to St Abb's Head turn right Ⓑ along a path, between a wire fence on the left and a wall on the right. After passing through a metal kissing-gate, the path turns left and later curves right to continue as a cliff-top route with superb views of the spectacular rocky coastline. The winding path is

clear and easy to follow, initially keeping to the cliff top, later descending into a grassy valley below the cliffs and ascending again to regain the cliff top.

Continue to the lighthouse on St Abb's Head, bear left Ⓒ, to pass to the left of the lighthouse cottage and descend to a tarmac road. Before you continue along the road, a brief detour along a narrow path up the small hill to the left provides a magnificent view along the Berwick-shire and Lothian coasts and inland to the Cheviots and across the Border country. Walk along the winding, narrow road, descending above Mire Loch and bending to the left.

Before reaching a cattle-grid, turn left Ⓓ across grass towards the loch, climb a stile to the left of a gate and continue along a pleasant winding path through reeds, gorse, rough grass and stunted trees. The path climbs steadily, and from it there are fine views to the left over Mire Loch and ahead to the sea. The loch is man-made, created by the building of a dam in 1900. On joining a track at the far end of the loch, turn right ⓔ uphill to rejoin the lighthouse road at a bend and keep ahead along it, following it around several bends to Northfield Farm ⓕ, a nature reserve centre. St Abb's Head is a National Nature Reserve, owned by the National Trust for Scotland and managed in co-operation with the Scottish Wildlife Trust. It is of national importance for its plant life and geology and especially as a nesting-place for large numbers of seabirds.

Turn left through the car park, walk past the picnic area and farm buildings to climb a stile onto a road and follow the road back through St Abbs, temporarily rejoining the outward route. After passing above the harbour, the outward route turns left along Murrayfield, but here keep straight ahead ⓐ along Creel Road. The road soon ends, but continue along a most attractive, grassy, undulating path, enclosed and later tree-lined, to reach a road.

Turn left along the road into the village of Coldingham, whose church incorporates parts of a medieval priory,

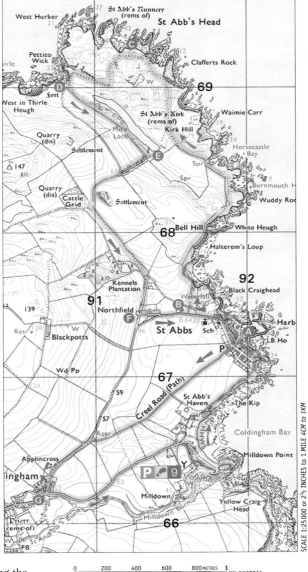

SCALE 1:25000 or 2½ INCHES TO 1 MILE 4CM to 1KM

originally founded in the 11th century and repeatedly attacked and damaged during the many wars between Scotland and England.

On the edge of the village, turn left ⓖ along a road signposted to Sands and follow it back to the start. For most of the way there is a parallel footpath to the left of the road. ●

Whiteadder valley and Edin's Hall Broch

Start	Abbey St Bathans
Distance	5 miles (8km)
Approximate time	2½ hours
Parking	Riverside car park nearly ½ mile (800m) south-east of church at Abbey St Bathans
Refreshments	Restaurant by car park
Ordnance Survey maps	Landranger 67 (Duns, Dunbar & Eyemouth), Explorer 345 (Lammermuir Hills)

An Iron Age broch spectacularly situated above the valley of Whiteadder Water is the main focal point of this relatively short and undemanding walk in the foothills of the Lammermuir Hills. The route is through or above the well-wooded valley with attractive riverside stretches, splendid views across the valley to the Lammermuirs and only a few modest climbs.

The origins of Abbey St Bathans are uncertain but there is alleged to have been a Christian settlement here since the 7th century, and the mainly 18th-century church, about ½ mile (800m) from the starting point, incorporates part of a medieval priory.

Start by walking up to the road and turn left along it, heading steadily uphill. At a right-hand bend, turn left Ⓐ through a gate, at a public footpath sign, onto a path that descends steeply to cross first a footbridge over Eller Burn and then a stile. Turn left beside the burn, but the path soon bears right and heads uphill across open grassland above the valley of Whiteadder Water to a gate. Go through, follow the direction of a waymark to the left and head downhill, by a wire fence on the left, towards the river. Go through another gate and turn right to continue by a wire fence on the right.

Look out for a yellow waymark on a fence post, which directs you to the left. Continue above a line of scrub and gorse on the left to reach the remains of Edin's Hall Broch Ⓑ, impressive both in their size and extent as well as for their superb position on the slopes of Cockburn Law, high above the wooded Whiteadder valley and looking towards the Lammermuir Hills. This was a large circular defensive structure of stone, one of the few such Iron Age brochs in southern Scotland, surrounded by a complex system of earthworks.

From the broch continue along a path that heads downhill across a field to a metal kissing-gate in a wall. Go through, continue by a wire fence bordering woodland on the left, climb a stile and keep ahead along a grassy ridge to another stile. Climb this, turn left downhill by a wall on the left and turn right in the field corner to continue

The impressive remains of Edin's Hall Broch

above the river, by a wire fence on the left. Follow the curve of the river to the right to enter trees and reach a gate. Go through, follow the path to the left to pass to the left of a cottage and bear left again to cross a rather shaky suspension footbridge over Whiteadder Water **C**. From the bridge there are dramatic views as the river flows through a virtual gorge at this point.

Walk along the track ahead, which bends right and continues through attractive woodland to a road **D**. Turn left along it for 1 mile (1.6km), heading steadily uphill, and at a sign 'Blakerston, The Retreat' turn left **E** along a tarmac drive. Where the drive turns left, keep ahead along a broad, walled track, which later winds downhill towards the river and becomes pleasantly tree-lined.

Before reaching the river, look out for a waymarked stile on the right, climb it and bear left along a path that soon curves right and heads uphill between gorse bushes to a gate. Go through, and the path winds through trees high above the river before descending to a track and footbridge. Turn left to cross the footbridge over the river and turn left again to return to the start. ●

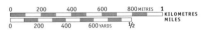

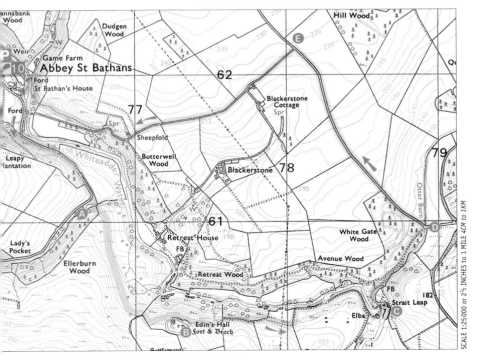

Hadrian's Wall from Steel Rigg

Start	Steel Rigg, 1 mile (1.6km) north of the National Park information centre at Once Brewed, Military Road, Bardon Mill
Distance	5 miles (8km)
Approximate time	2½ hours
Parking	National Park car park at Steel Rigg
Refreshments	None
Ordnance Survey maps	Landrangers 86 (Haltwhistle & Brampton) and 87 (Hexham & Haltwhistle), Explorer OL43 (Hadrian's Wall - Haltwhistle & Hexham)

This walk provides an opportunity to see the most dramatic stretch of Hadrian's Wall. Choose your time to undertake the route carefully – it is wise to avoid bank holiday afternoons! Early mornings or evenings are ideal, the low light dramatising the landscape and highlighting beautiful Crag Lough. Also avoid windy days. The return leg on the north side of Hadrian's Wall is pleasant walking, with wonderful views of the wall and the whinstone ridge on which it was built.

Pass through the kissing-gate in the lower right corner of the car park and follow the path to the wall at Peel Gap. Steps help the steep ascent to Peel Crags, which is the start of a series of switchback climbs and descents along perhaps the most photographed section of Hadrian's Wall. The spectacular view is of great interest geologically and strategically: the scarp of the Great Whin Sill is seen rising precipitously above Crag Lough while the dip slope falls gently away to the south. Look back too at the climb you have just made. It started from a vulnerable point in the wall – a gap where the Romans protected the wall by digging a deep ditch on its northern side. This can still be clearly seen.

The path soon descends again, to a gap known as Cat Stairs, where there is a tumble of stones that have fallen from the wall through the ages. The abundance of wild flowers on this rocky habitat is attributed to the mortar that was used in the construction of the wall, its lime modifying the composition of the soil. Another climb follows – and then a further steep descent, this time to Castle Nick.

The gap here was protected by Milecastle 39, which has been recently excavated. Although there are minor deviations in size and design, all of the milecastles along the wall had basic features in common. Built to accommodate eight soldiers, they were gatehouses allowing access from one side of

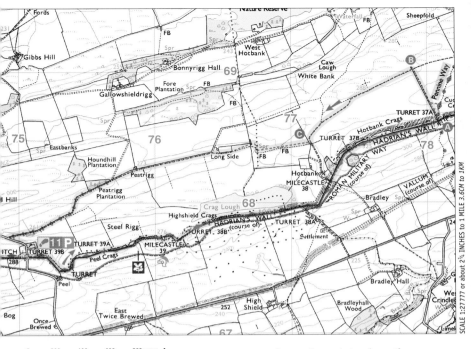

SCALE 1:27777 or about 2¼ INCHES to 1 MILE 3.6CM to 1KM

the wall to the other. Thus the most important feature was the gatetower itself, where the gates opened outwards on the north side of the wall. There were also living-quarters, a storehouse, an oven and, in the north-east corner, steps leading to the battlemented parapet of the wall itself, which was generally at least 19½ft (5.9m) high. All this was surrounded on the south side by an enclosing bailey wall, also with parapet walk and crenellations and a gate on its south side. As the name implies, milecastles were situated one Roman mile apart, about 1618 yds (1479m).

The path climbs again and then drops down steps to a circular stone wall, which protects an unhealthy-looking sycamore tree. Pass to the north side of the wall, following the waymarks. You are soon on the crags high above the lough. Heather-topped Barcombe Hill to the south is where the stone used in the wall was quarried. The communications

tower to the north-west stands on the hill memorably named Hopealone.

The path descends through National Trust woodland – planted, not a natural feature – and skirts the boundary of Hotbank Farm before a taxing climb alongside the wall up to Hotbank Crags. The view from the top is a classic – one often used to illustrate Hadrian's Wall on postcards and brochures. To the west the wall snakes its way towards the horizon above the sparkling waters of Crag Lough – on a clear day the Lakeland summits of Blencathra and Skiddaw can be seen. To the north are the twin Greenlee and Broomlee loughs, and Housesteads car park can be seen ahead, heralding the most popular part of Hadrian's Wall.

For a short distance the wall is unreconstructed, and the path alongside dips down sharply to Ranishaw Gap, which is where the Pennine Way joins with the wall to follow it westwards. A gate Ⓐ and steps are on the left. Cross the wall by these but do not follow the waymark that points out the course of the Pennine Way towards Broomlee Lough north-eastwards. Instead, follow the line of a broken-down wall, keeping it to the left, so that you are walking directly away from Hadrian's Wall at this point. At what looks like an ornate cattle-shelter **B**, but was in fact a lime-kiln, turn left to follow a small escarpment westwards.

On the left is a planting of conifers, and Greenlee Lough is on the right. Hadrian's Wall from here looks a forbidding defence-work; it must have deterred many a raiding party. The walking is easy on springy turf. Another path joins from the right as ours bends to the left and turns again to reach a stone wall and a farm gate **C**. Turn to the right, following a waymark pointing across a large pasture, where a notice requests people to walk in single file to avoid damaging the hay crop. From here the cliffs rearing above Crag Lough are truly impressive.

Cross the next meadow, following a well-used but still grassy path towards the crags on top of Steel Rigg. The path bends to the right to cross slightly boggy ground to reach a gate. Use the adjacent ladder-stile and follow the right-of-way, which now heads towards a byre, keeping close to the wall on the right. Almost imperceptibly the path becomes a track. Pass Peatrigg Plantation and continue along the track until it reaches the road below Steel Rigg car park and turn left to return to the starting point.

Hadrian's Wall from Peel Crags

Kelso, Roxburgh and the River Teviot

Start	Kelso
Distance	8 miles (12.9km). Shorter version 3½ miles (5.6km)
Approximate time	4 hours (1½ hours for shorter version)
Parking	Kelso
Refreshments	Pubs and cafés at Kelso
Ordnance Survey maps	Landranger 74 (Kelso & Coldstream), Explorer 339 (Kelso, Coldstream & Lower Tweed Valley)

The River Teviot is one of the main tributaries of the River Tweed, and this walk follows a particularly attractive stretch of it from near the confluence of the two rivers at Kelso, past the fragmentary remains of the once powerful Roxburgh Castle, to the disused railway viaduct by Roxburgh village. Although this 'there and back' route is quite long, the going is easy along clear and well-waymarked paths.

With a spacious cobbled square lined by dignified buildings and dominated by a Classical town hall, with its fine position on the north bank of the River Tweed crossed here by an elegant bridge built by Rennie in 1803, and the remains of a medieval abbey, Kelso is one of the most attractive and interesting Border towns. Kelso Abbey was founded by David I in 1128 but fell victim to repeated English invasions and was finally destroyed in 1545. Only the west tower and western transepts remain standing to their full height but they clearly reveal the magnificence of what was the largest of the Border abbeys.

Start in the Square, face the town hall and turn right along Bridge Street, passing the abbey ruins. Cross Kelso Bridge, and to the right is a view of the vast 18th- to 19th-century Floors Castle, seat of the dukes of Roxburghe. Turn right Ⓐ beside the Tweed, along

the road signposted to St Boswells and Selkirk, and after passing the confluence of the two rivers continue beside the Teviot.

Follow the road to the right to cross the bridge over the Teviot and, just after passing a cottage on the left, turn left over a stone stile Ⓑ and turn right along a path that shortly descends steps to the river. Continue along a riverside path and, after bending left, you pass below the scanty remains of Roxburgh Castle, once a powerful royal residence occupying a ridge between the Teviot and Tweed and guarding the important Royal Burgh of Roxburgh. In such a strategic Border area, Roxburgh was continually attacked by English armies and frequently changed hands between Scotland and England. James II of Scotland was killed by the bursting of a cannon while trying to recapture the castle from the English in 1460, and

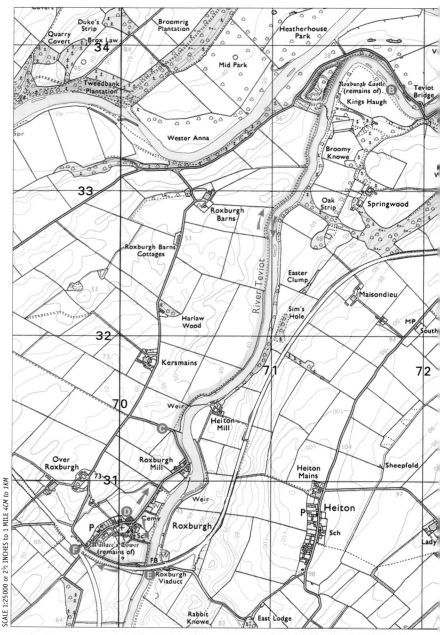

shortly afterwards his widow ordered it
to be dismantled. The town was later
destroyed by Edward VI in 1550 and it
has now entirely vanished; the present
village of the same name is on a
different site. From the castle mound
there is a particularly impressive view
of Floors Castle.

*Those doing the shorter version
should return by retracing their steps
from here.*

Continue along the riverside path,
a most attractive route, tree-lined in
places and with fine open views across
the surrounding countryside. Look out
for where you turn right through a gate

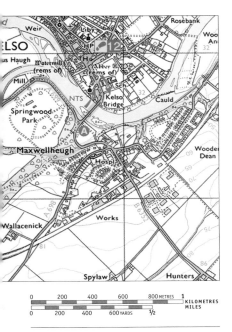

```
0      200    400    600    800 METRES   1
                                         KILOMETRES
                                         MILES
0      200    400    600 YARDS   ½
```

– immediately after climbing a stile –
then turn left to continue along the left-
hand edge of a field above the river,
eventually following the field edge

round to the right and turning left over
a stile onto a lane **C**.

Turn left along the lane into
Roxburgh and, on the edge of the
village, turn left along a track **D**. The
track turns left towards the river and
then bends to the right to follow the
Teviot up to the impressive but disused
railway viaduct. In front of the viaduct,
turn right **E** along a track that heads
gently uphill, between the wooded
railway embankment on the left and a
hedge on the right, to a road. The ruins
seen in the field on the right are of
Wallace's Tower, allegedly the remnant
of a 13th-century tower built by the
Scottish patriot William Wallace.

Turn right **F** through the village,
passing the sturdy-looking 18th-
century church, to rejoin the outward
route and retrace your steps to Kelso. ●

*Kelso's five-arched bridge, designed by John
Rennie in 1803*

Above Rothbury

Start	Rothbury
Distance	5 miles (8km)
Approximate time	3 hours
Parking	Riverside picnic site on the west side of Rothbury on B6341
Refreshments	Pubs and cafés in Rothbury
Ordnance Survey maps	Landranger 81 (Alnwick & Morpeth), Explorer 332 (Alnwick & Amble)

Rothbury is a favourite centre for walkers wishing to explore the heart of Northumberland. The town is built on a series of natural, south-facing terraces overlooking the River Coquet. Above the town some of the higher terraces were adapted by Lord Armstrong as carriage-drives after he built Cragside; this walk uses parts of these. After the initial stiff climb, the walking is mainly easy and varied with fine views over the town and valley.

Take the path up to the road from the middle of the picnic site. Turn right to the County Hotel and then sharp left up a road that makes a gentle ascent of the hill (Beggars Rigg), giving good views of the valley. Continue past Hillside Road on the right to the houses where the road levels. Look for a bungalow called Roding on the right. Between Roding and its neighbouring house, Midmar, stone steps set into the road-side wall lead to a well-concealed foot-path Ⓐ that runs between the gardens of the two properties. Initially, this path is narrow, but when it has climbed beyond the gardens – through thickish bracken in summer – it becomes a pleasant route up the hillside, passing through a copse before coming to a wall above the quarry. Climb over the wall and skirt around the bottom of the field above the quarries to reach a track that goes to Gimmerknowe, a cottage that can be seen on the left. Bear right, go

through the gate at the top Ⓑ and turn left onto a pleasant track leading below Ship Crag towards woodland. Pass Whinhause (the house formerly called Brae Head) on the left, still climbing.

After Physic Lane joins the route from Thropton on the left, the stone wall on that side gradually bends away to the west. A clump of trees is passed on the left – continue straight on along the main track at this point.

Turn to the left at the next opportunity – a major crossways Ⓒ – around the shoulder of the hill. A wonderful panorama opens up at this point, with the remains of Cartington Castle amidst trees to the left. This dates from the early 14th century though its licence to crenellate was granted later, in 1441. A century after this, it was described as being 'a good fortresse of two toures and other strange houses'. In 1648 it suffered from coming under fire by Parliamentary forces. The siege lasted

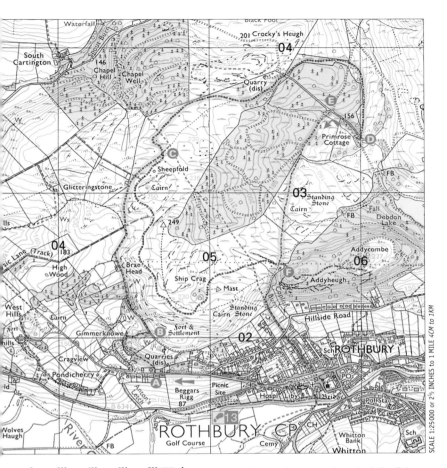

SCALE 1:25000 or 2½ INCHES to 1 MILE 4CM to 1KM

```
0      200    400    600    800 METRES   1
                                         KILOMETRES
                                         MILES
0      200    400    600 YARDS    ½
```

for just two hours but left the castle in ruins. In the distance beyond Cartington the long shape of the Cheviot can be identified, with Hedgehope to its right.

A little further and the track arrives at the corner of the timber planting and then descends gently to more woodland. Cross another track, following the footpath signed to Primrose Cottage. This is a delightful section with woods to the right and views down to Debdon on the left. The path dips down to Primrose Cottage **D**, passing beehives. Turn sharply to the right here, passing through the gate and following a track leading steeply uphill through the wood.

Keep a sharp watch to the left of the track, looking for a stile **E** and gate with a signpost to Rothbury. This path threads past pines and beech trees until another footpath sign on the left points to a stile that takes it out of the wood onto the moor again. Head for the radio mast ahead, looking for an ancient parish boundary stone by the wayside as the path threads through the heather, descending to the bottom of the wood on the left. It crosses another footpath, which emerges from the wood. Turn right at this point **F** if you wish to reach the best viewpoint – the cairn marked on the map – otherwise continue on the downward path towards Rothbury, with the wood on the left. The views to the south, over the town and river to the dark ridge of the

Simonside Hills, are truly memorable. These hills, of fell sandstone, have distinctive outlines that have been compared to breaking waves. The outlying summits are Dove Crag to the left and Raven's Heugh to the right. Cross Hillside Road and resume the descent to the town, emerging at its centre.

Here refreshment can be found in a variety of hostelries, or you can continue on the route, passing the National Park information centre and the church on the left. There is a footpath leading down steps to the riverside walk by the lamp-post beyond the church (a graveyard is on the right). Turn right onto the riverside walk and, having passed the gardens of the County Hotel, look for a path on the right that leads up to the picnic site starting point. ●

The River Coquet near Rothbury

Peebles and
the River Tweed

Start	Peebles
Distance	7½ miles (12.1km). Shorter version 4 miles (6.4km)
Approximate time	3½ hours (2 hours for shorter version)
Parking	Peebles
Refreshments	Pubs and cafés at Peebles
Ordnance Survey maps	Landranger 73 (Peebles, Galashiels & Selkirk), Explorer 337 (Peebles & Innerleithen) and 338 (Galashiels, Selkirk & Melrose)

Much fine riverside walking is to be found on this well-waymarked route, which explores some of the most attractive stretches of the Tweed valley to the west of Peebles, mostly using riverside and field paths, woodland tracks and part of a disused railway line. The first half of the walk follows the north bank of the river upstream, passing below Neidpath Castle, to Manor Bridge and on to Lyne Bridge. The return is along the south side of the valley, and there are fine views all the way. The shorter version only goes as far as Manor Bridge.

'Peebles for pleasure' states the old saying, and the town is certainly an excellent touring and walking centre, situated on the banks of the River Tweed and surrounded by wooded hills and open moorlands. It has a good range of shops, eating-places, hotels and guesthouses as well as attractive riverside gardens and a promenade. Peebles is an ancient town, once an important ecclesiastical centre, although there is not much evidence of this apart from the tower of a 12th-century collegiate church and the remains of a friary, Cross Kirk, founded by Alexander III in 1261. These lie in a peaceful and secluded setting on the north side of the town. The friary became the parish church until being abandoned in 1783, and its Victorian successor is situated at the top end of

High Street, its tower and crown spire dominating most of the views of the town.

Start by this church and turn down towards the river. Do not cross Tweed Bridge but turn right down a tarmac drive, passing to the right of a swimming-pool and on to join a riverside path. Cross a footbridge over a tributary stream and continue by the Tweed through Haylodge Park, passing a metal footbridge (Victoria Bridge).

At the end of the park, continue along the riverside path to Neidpath Viaduct. This is a delightful stretch of the walk: the Tweed flows between steep, thickly wooded banks, while the path dips up and down and passes below the ruins of Neidpath Castle in a dramatic situation above the river. The castle is essentially a 14th-century

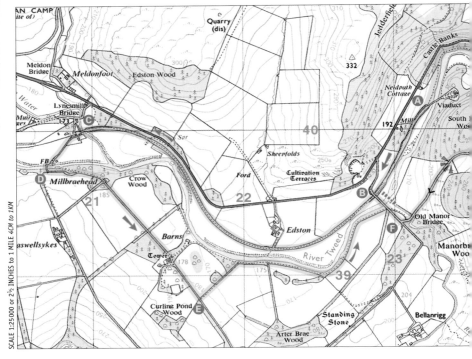

tower-house, modernised in the 17th century. It was besieged and captured by Cromwell's armies in 1650.

At the disused viaduct Ⓐ, climb a stile to the right of it, go up steps and bear right at the top, in the 'Tweed Walk, Lyne Station' direction, to continue along the bed of the former railway track. The track eventually descends to go through a gate onto a road just to the right of Manor Bridge Ⓑ.

The shorter version turns left over the bridge and rejoins the full walk on the other side.

Cross the road, climb the stile opposite, climb steps to rejoin the disused railway track and continue along it, climbing several stiles. After crossing a bridge over Lyne Water, turn left down steps to a lane Ⓒ and turn right along it. The tarmac lane soon becomes a rough track, and at a fork take the right-hand path that leads to a footbridge over the Tweed. Turn left over the bridge and turn left again Ⓓ along a path that keeps along the edge of

riverside woodland and continues through trees to a track. Bear right along the gently ascending track and, after passing the end of a road, keep ahead along a straight, tree-lined track. The track later keeps along the left inside edge of woodland and emerges

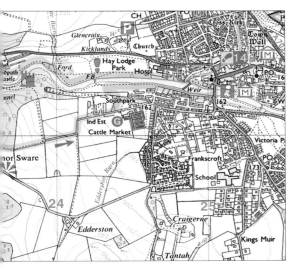

field, by a wall on the left. Head down to climb a stile, continue along a track to climb another one and turn right to keep along the south bank of the river. Now comes another delightful stretch of riverside walking across tree-fringed meadows, climbing several stiles, to reach Manor Bridge again.

Turn right up steps beside the bridge, climb a stile onto the road and turn right along it. Take the first turning on the left **F**, cross Old Manor Brig, dated 1702, and continue along an uphill lane. Behind there are lovely views of the Tweed valley. At a Tweed Walk sign near the top, turn left beside a gate and, at a fork a few yards ahead, take the right-hand path, between a wall on the right and a wire fence bordering woodland on the left to reach a stile. At this point there is a superb view of Peebles ahead, lying in the valley backed by the surrounding wooded hills. Climb the stile, head downhill along the right-hand edge of a field, by a wall and later a wire fence on the right, climb another stile and continue along an enclosed track, following it around left- and right-hand bends to join a tarmac road.

from the trees to pass Barns Tower, a 15th-century peel tower – beyond is its 18th-century successor, the more comfortable and elegant Barns House.

Continue along the track as far as a Tweed Walk footpath sign, which directs you to turn left **E** over a stile and walk along the left-hand edge of a

Approaching Peebles

Walk along the road and, after passing two side-roads on the left that both lead into a small industrial estate, turn left **G** through a kissing-gate into a field and walk across it to a way-marked stile at the far, narrow end. Climb the stile, take the path ahead, go through a gate and continue down to reach the river opposite Victoria Bridge. Turn right along the tarmac riverside path to return to the start. ●

Arnton Fell

Start	Second layby on the right – it has a seat – along the lane to Steele Road, ¾ mile (1.2km) from the B6399
Distance	5½ miles (8.9km)
Approximate time	3 hours
Parking	At layby
Refreshments	None
Ordnance Survey maps	Landranger 79 (Hawick & Eskdale), Explorer OL42 (Kielder Water & Forest - Bellingham & Simonside Hills)

Both on the long, gradual ascent of Arnton Fell and the return route along its lower slopes, there are superb views of Liddesdale with the formidable walls of Hermitage Castle standing out prominently. This is a most enjoyable and exhilarating walk, partly on rough moorland paths and partly on easy tracks, in one of the loneliest and most remote parts of the Borders – indeed amidst such bleak and empty expanses it is best not to attempt it in poor visibility.

Almost opposite the layby there is a stile beside a gate with a Roman helmet waymark. Climb it, immediately bear left off the track ahead and walk across grass to keep alongside a wire fence on the right. Where the fence turns right,

Liddesdale from the slopes of Arnton Fell

continue along the left edge of Steele Plantation to a stile, climb it – here rejoining the fence – and head steadily uphill beside it onto the open grassy slopes of Arnton Fell.

Go through a gate, continue along the uphill path, bearing left away from the fence and climbing more steeply to reach a triangulation pillar. From here walk along the superb, broad, grassy summit ridge to a cairn by a fence corner **Ⓐ**. The magnificent all-round views from this point take in Liddesdale, Newcastleton, Hermitage Castle, the Cheviots and the Border Forest. Continue on an undula-ting route beside a wire fence on the right for just over 1 mile (1.6km), keeping beside a plantation on the right to where the fence bordering the plantation bends sharply to the right **B**.

At this point, turn left and, with Hermitage Castle directly ahead, descend steeply across rough grass to reach a track **C**. Turn left and follow it for 2 miles (3.2km) to a lane. It is a winding track that goes through several gates and past Roughley Farm to reach a ford over Watt's Burn. Look for a small, grassed over quarry on the left and veer uphill at an angle of 45 degrees. Come

round the flank of the hill and head towards the corner of a small wood, going through a gate in the electric fence.

Walk past this wood then head towards the far corner of another wood. Go through a gate in the deer fence then veer left, slightly uphill and follow the line of the wood until you intersect a well defined path **D** which will take you back to the start. ●

SCALE 1:26 316 or 2½ INCHES to 1 MILE 3.8CM to 1KM

Hadrian's Wall: Vindolanda and Housesteads (vertical sidebar text)

Hadrian's Wall: Vindolanda and Housesteads

Start	Housesteads Fort
Distance	7 miles (11.3km)
Approximate time	4½ hours
Parking	Housesteads
Refreshments	Cafés at Vindolanda and Housesteads
Ordnance Survey maps	Landrangers 86 (Haltwhistle & Brampton) and 87 (Hexham & Haltwhistle), Explorer OL43 (Hadrian's Wall - Haltwhistle & Hexham)

This walk links the two most popular, interesting and best-preserved Hadrian's Wall forts, one on the wall itself and the other just to the south of it. In between you cross the open grassland and heath of Thorngrafton Common and walk along the edge of a delightful wooded valley, but the highlight comes towards the end – a short walk along what is arguably the most dramatic and impressive stretch of Hadrian's Wall. There is plenty of 'up and down' work and some rough and potentially muddy going at times but the extensive views and tremendous sense of history combine to create a most absorbing and exhilarating walk.

Start in front of the Visitor Centre and facing the road, go through a gate, climb a stile and head up to the road. Turn right and after nearly ½ mile (800m) turn left over a ladder-stile, at a public bridleway sign, and follow the direction of the sign across a field, first heading downhill and then continuing up over a brow.

Bear right, heading down and up again, and then follow a track down to a farm. Pass through the farmyard and continue along a tarmac track that bears left up to a lane. Turn right and take the first turning on the left, sign-posted to Thorngrafton and Bardon Mill. At a public footpath sign to West End Town, turn right over a stone stile

Ⓐ and follow a curving and undulating path across the rough grassland and heath of Thorngrafton Common to a ladder-stile. After climbing it, look out for a stile in a wire fence just in front of a small burn. Climb that, cross the burn and continue in the same direction across the common – there is a faint but discernible path – making for a ladder-stile in a wall. Ahead are superb views over the South Tyne valley.

Climb the ladder-stile and continue in the same direction towards another one. After climbing that, keep ahead, roughly parallel with a wall on the left,

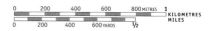

later veering right and away from it to climb a ladder-stile onto an enclosed track. Turn left down to a junction and turn right – not along the track to West End Town Farm but along a lower track parallel to it – to go through a metal kissing-gate. Pass in front of the farmhouse and, at a wall corner on the left, bear left off the track and head downhill to join and keep beside the left bank of a burn. Continue between gateposts, keep beside a hedge and fence on the right and climb a stone stile onto a lane .

Turn right, take the first turning on the left, cross a bridge over Chainley Burn and, at a T-junction, turn right, in the Vindolanda and Once Brewed direction, heading uphill. Where the lane

curves left, turn right over a stone stile, at a public footpath sign to Vindolanda and Hadrian's Wall . Walk along a track and, just after passing a barn, bear left to a stile. Climb it and follow a track above the wooded valley of Chainley Burn to Vindolanda, going over stiles and through gates and, at one point, crossing a footbridge over a side burn just below a farm. In the latter stages the track keeps beside the burn and crosses a footbridge over it just before reaching the entrance to the Vindolanda Museum.

The museum is surrounded by attractive ornamental gardens that slope down to the burn and contain various replica Roman buildings. Inside there is an outstanding collection of finds from the site that include items of pottery, household goods, tools, agricultural implements, weapons, clothing

A spectacular view of Hadrian's Wall near Housesteads

and shoes. There are even fragments of letters, including a note from one soldier to another enquiring if there are any decent pubs in the locality!

The fort itself lies to the west of the museum and occupies a plateau above the valley of Chainley Burn. It was one of the auxiliary forts on the Stanegate, a road that ran parallel and a little to the south of Hadrian's Wall, and is of the usual playing-card shape that was common to all Roman forts throughout the empire. Originally built of timber in the 1st century AD, it was rebuilt in stone in both the 2nd and 3rd centuries. Excavation is a continuing process, and the foundations and parts of the walls of the outer defences, gateways and various buildings of the fort can be traced, along with those of the sizeable civilian settlement or vicus that grew up outside the west wall. In addition there is a modern reconstruction of a short section of both stone and turf wall, together with a timber milecastle.

From the entrance to the museum, the route continues to the right, heading uphill alongside the ornamental gardens and then along a tarmac drive to a lane. Turn left and, immediately after recrossing the burn, turn right over a ladder-stile, by a Roman milestone and a public footpath sign to High Shield **D**. Don't take the track beside the burn but bear slightly left up through a small group of trees and continue uphill across a field. Behind is an excellent view of Vindolanda.

Over the brow, make for the right-hand corner of the field, where you climb a stile. Continue uphill along the right edge of the next field, climb a ladder-stile, keep ahead along a track to the right of farm buildings and turn right over a stile. Bear slightly left and walk diagonally across a field to climb a stone stile onto a road. Turn right and after ¼ mile (400m), turn left through a gate at a public footpath sign and National Trust sign Hotbank Farm. Walk along a track and at a public footpath sign to Housesteads Fort, turn right over a ladder-stile onto the path beside Hadrian's Wall **E**.

You now follow a switchback route beside the wall to the fort at Housesteads, a distance of just over 1 mile (1.6km). There are a number of ladder-stiles to climb and several quite steep ascents and descents, but the extensive views – on both sides and along the length of the wall – are magnificent. To the right is the valley of the South Tyne and the distant line of the Pennines; to the left across Crag Lough, Greenlee Lough and Broomlee Lough the dark outlines of the Border forest can be seen; and ahead stretches the wall, keeping to the highest ground all the while. Shortly after passing to the right of Housesteads Milecastle, the route takes to the top of the wall itself, passing through a belt of trees to reach the fort. Turn right over a stone stile **F** to leave the wall and keep beside the west wall of the fort down to the south-west corner.

Housesteads (or Vercovicium) is the most complete and fully excavated of the 17 wall forts. Like Vindolanda it is of the usual playing-card shape, best appreciated from below, and the wall itself forms the north side of the fort. In the middle stands the *principia* or head-quarters' building and around it are the extensive foundations of the granaries, commandant's house, barracks and a well-preserved latrine. The latter enables you to appreciate the high standards of cleanliness and personal hygiene enjoyed, even in this most northerly outpost of the Roman Empire.

From the fort, head down to a path to the left of the museum and at a fork take the left-hand path that winds downhill back to the start. ●

Melrose and the Eildon Hills

Start	Melrose
Distance	5½ miles (8.9km)
Approximate time	3 hours
Parking	Melrose
Refreshments	Pubs and cafés at Melrose
Ordnance Survey maps	Landranger 73 (Peebles, Galashiels & Selkirk), Explorer 337 (Peebles & Innerleithen) and 338 (Galashiels, Selkirk & Melrose)

From almost all parts of the Border country, and indeed from a high proportion of the other walks in this book, the distinctive three peaks of the Eildon Hills can be seen, rising abruptly like a mini-mountain range above the Tweed valley. This walk climbs the two highest of these three peaks, both magnificent viewpoints, and after a steep descent into the village of Newstead finishes off with an attractive and relaxing stroll beside the River Tweed. Although not rising to any great height, the ascent of the Eildons is quite steep and tiring, but the paths are good, the route is well waymarked and the extensive views over Melrose, the Tweed valley and much of the Border country more than compensate for the effort. Leave plenty of time to visit Melrose Abbey, one of the finest monastic ruins in the country.

The pleasant, small town of Melrose is dominated by the beautiful and extensive ruins of its abbey, built of the local pink sandstone and occupying a lovely setting on the south bank of the Tweed below the Eildons. The history of Melrose Abbey largely mirrors that of the other Border abbeys: founded by David I in 1136, repeatedly attacked and devastated by invading English armies and left in ruins after the last of these raids in the 1540s. It is, however, more complete and better preserved than most, especially the mainly 14th- and 15th-century church, the finest example in Scotland of the ornate Decorated style. The cloisters and domestic buildings are on the north side of the church, not as usual on the sunnier south side, probably because it was easier to use water from the Tweed for drainage and other purposes.

This is an easy route to follow as it is well-waymarked throughout with yellow arrows and 'Eildon Walk' signs. Start in Market Square and take the road signposted to Lilliesleaf, heading uphill and passing under the bypass bridge. About 100 yds (91m) past the bridge, turn left **Ⓐ** at an Eildon Walk sign, go down steps and take the narrow uphill path ahead alongside the left-hand edge of woodland. Bear right to ascend a long flight of steps and climb a stile at the top of them.

Head uphill, between wire fences,

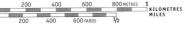

SCALE 1:25 000 or 2½ INCHES to 1 MILE 4CM to 1KM

climb two stiles in quick succession and continue up along the left-hand edge of a field, by a wire fence on the left, climbing another stile to emerge onto the open hillside. Keep ahead to a footpath sign and turn right along a winding, steadily ascending path that reaches the gap between the North and Mid peaks of the Eildons. At a footpath sign, keep ahead for 50 yds (46m) to a crossing of paths **B** and turn right for the steep ascent of Mid Hill (1385ft/ 422m). At the summit **C**, a view-indicator enables you to appreciate the tremendous panorama spread out

Melrose Abbey

before you. To the south is Wester Hill, the lowest of the three peaks at 1216ft (369m).

Retrace your steps to the crossing of paths **B** and continue ahead to follow a clear, broad, winding track across heathery moorland up to the summit of North Hill (1323ft/404m) **D**, a steady and less steep ascent. At the top are the remains of an Iron Age fort and a Roman signal station as well as another magnificent view, which includes Melrose down in the valley below, the winding Tweed, Mid and Wester hills and a large slice of the Border country.

At the summit cairn, bear left to continue along the ridge and at a fork take the left-hand path – narrow but clear – that descends steeply between gorse and heather, making for a conifer plantation below. On reaching the conifers, keep along their left-hand edge down to a stile, climb it and continue down an enclosed, hedge- and tree-lined path to a road. Turn right, take the first track on the left **E** and follow it gently down, passing

under a disused railway bridge, to a T-junction. Turn right along a track and turn left down Claymires Lane to the road in the village of Newstead **F**.

Cross the road, continue along a tarmac track opposite – it later becomes a rough track – heading downhill, cross a footbridge over a narrow stream and shortly bear left to join the Tweed. Climb a stile and keep alongside the river, a most attractive stretch with fine views upstream. After the next stile you have to walk on top of a wall, known as the Battery Dyke – take care as it is quite narrow – and where the wall peters out, continue along a pleasant, partially tree- and hedge-lined path. To the left are attractive views of the Eildons and Melrose Abbey, and upstream a suspension bridge can be seen.

After going through a metal gate, immediately turn left **G** along the left-hand edge of a field, by a fence and hedge on the left, and go through a kissing-gate onto a lane. Turn left to a T-junction and turn right along a road, passing the entrance to the abbey and returning to Market square. ●

Hadrian's Wall at Walltown and Thirlwall Castle

Hadrian's Wall at Walltown and Thirlwall Castle

Start	Walltown, north of Military Road (B6318), 1 mile (1.6km) east of Greenhead
Distance	7½ miles (12.1km). Shorter version 4½ miles (7.2km)
Approximate time	4 hours (2½ hours for shorter version)
Parking	National Park car park just before Walltown Farm
Refreshments	Tearoom at Holmhead, opposite Thirlwall Castle
Ordnance Survey maps	Landrangers 86 (Haltwhistle & Brampton) and 87 (Hexham & Haltwhistle), Explorer OL43 (Hadrian's Wall - Haltwhistle & Hexham)

This section of Hadrian's Wall is one of the most spectacular but is seldom as crowded as those further east. After a 2-mile (3.2km) walk along the wall a return is made by the vallum, the defensive ditch built to the south of the wall, which also provided an easy corridor of communication along its length. The longer walk provides an opportunity to appreciate the wall from an attacker's viewpoint and to see a later defensive structure, the medieval Thirlwall Castle. If the weather has been wet, take care in using the stepping-stones across the Tipalt Burn.

From the parking-space take the path up to Hadrian's Wall, which here crosses the Nine Nicks of Thirlwall, though only five 'nicks' are to be seen today. They are short gaps in the crag, which the Romans had to overcome in building their wall. Four have been lost because of quarrying. Although the route of the walk lies eastwards, it is worth climbing the short length to the west **Ⓐ** to take in the magnificent view over the quarry towards the hills of Cumbria. As we shall see on the last lap of the walk, the County Council are reclaiming Walltown Quarry, which was an important source of whinstone for road surfaces until 1978.

Turn back eastwards, following the wall. This short section incorporates up to fourteen courses of original stone-work, making it one of the best-preserved stretches. Chives and other medicinal herbs flourish here, and it may be that these derive from seeds sown by legionaries. Because of this it was a location much frequented by Elizabethan herbalists. The fabric of the wall deteriorates after the remains of Turret 45A – which is unusual in having been built before the wall itself. The turrets were spaced between the larger milecastles, about a third of a Roman mile apart. It seems most likely that they were primarily look-out posts, being manned by detachments from the milecastles.

The descent to Walltown Nick is steep, as is the climb on the other side.

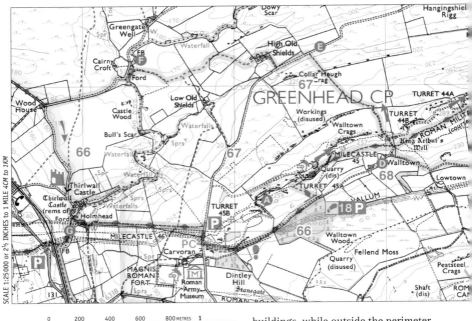

The wall follows the rising and falling ground eastwards like a switchback and makes for energetic walking. Little of its fabric survives above ground. It passes Allolee, plunging down before climbing steeply to the site of Milecastle 44 on the other side. These small forts were set at intervals of a Roman mile along the wall and provided access through the wall as well as accommodation for a small platoon of soldiers.

There is a more gentle descent to the next farmstead, Cockmount Hill, which is sheltered by a planting of conifers. The path passes through the trees and past the front of the house to reach the giant cattle-sheds at Great Chesters, where there was an important Roman command centre at the fort known as Aesica. The most interesting feature of Aesica is at its centre, surrounded by a fence. This is the entry to the vaulted underground strongroom of the garrison, which held the soldiers' pay. The fort also had its own granary and shrines as well as administrative buildings, while outside the perimeter, in the field to the east, were situated the bath-house, steam-room and latrines. The water to service this complex, built in AD 128, was brought by aqueduct from a stream more than 2 miles (3.2km) away. However, to maintain the correct rate of flow the aqueduct was 6 miles (9.7km) long – a remarkable feat of engineering.

Turn right here **B**, away from the farm down its drive, and then right again **C** to follow the course of the vallum along an unclassified county road. *Vallum* is the Latin for 'wall', but in this instance it is a defensive ditch about 130ft (40m) wide. The mistake is said to have originated from the writings of the Venerable Bede. The vallum marked the beginning of the military zone but there were causeways across it guarded by gates that gave access to milecastles.

The vallum gives an excellent view of Hadrian's Wall from the south – even from this aspect it looks formidable. The track leaves the vallum at Blake Law and joins the drive from Allolee. It crosses a cattle-grid and passes an old

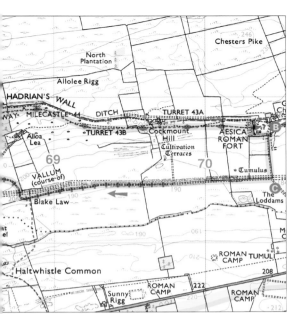

through this and make for the white cottage with three pine trees. There is a ladder-stile over the wall ahead; after this, descend through the next meadow, still heading for Cairny Croft. The Tipalt Burn lies between you and the road and has to be crossed by stepping-stones, which is easy enough in dry spells but may be hazardous if it is in spate.

Turn left onto the road. There is a lovely view back as it climbs steadily uphill. Turn left at the junction and descend to Thirlwall Castle, taking the rough farm track by the ruins. The castle was built of stone taken from Hadrian's Wall, which accounts for there being little trace of the wall above ground in the vicinity. Edward I is supposed to have slept at Thirlwall in 1306 though other accounts give the date of its completion forty years later. Although it was lived in until the 18th century, it was already dilapidated in 1542. Legend has it that a ghostly dwarf guards the castle's treasure – a table made of solid gold. The track leads down to the Tipalt Burn, which is crossed this time by a foot-bridge at a delightful spot, Holmhead. There is a cottage overlooking the stream here, which provides refreshments for hikers as this part of the walk is also a section of the Pennine Way.

Bear left up the steep slope to reach the vallum. This is a magnificent stretch which climbs steeply up the hill. Turn right at the lane to pass the newly landscaped Walltown Quarry, then left onto the footpath along its edge to return to the start of the walk. ●

quarry-working. King Arthur's Well, a hill-fort from pre-Roman times, is seen ahead, to the right.

For the shorter walk, follow the road back past Walltown Farm to the starting point.

To continue on the longer walk, turn to the right just before the farm ⒟ and climb to the wall again at the declivity below King Arthur's Well.

From here the path heads north-west over rather soggy ground, along what seems to be an ancient paved way. Pass through a muddy gateway and fork left on what looks suspiciously like a sheep-track. The road can soon be seen in the distance on the right. Head for the stone wall and from here look for a stile over the next wall, just to the right of the roof of High Old Shield (binoculars would be handy).

Cross this stile and a small footbridge to reach the road ⒠ and turn left. Walk up the drive of High Old Shield and pass to the right of the house and round the back of it through two farmyard gates so that you emerge on the west side of the house. Now head for the gate in the stone wall at the bottom of the field. Go

Windy Gyle

Start	Near Windyhaugh about 6 miles (9.7km) upstream from Alwinton
Distance	7 miles (11.3km)
Approximate time	4½ hours
Parking	Where Rowhope Burn joins the River Coquet just north-west of Windyhaugh
Refreshments	None
Ordnance Survey maps	Landranger 80 (Cheviot Hills & Kielder Water), Explorer OL16 (The Cheviot Hills)

For some reason gloomy names have been attached to many of the features encountered on this walk – Dreary Sike, The Slime, Foul Step – yet this should put no one off from experiencing the splendour of Windy Gyle. The summit, Russell's Cairn, is an incomparable viewpoint on a fine day – but this is not a route to be undertaken in adverse conditions. The walk up to this part of the Pennine Way has relatively easy gradients even though they seem to go on for a long way. Much of the surrounding land serves as a Ministry of Defence Dry Training Area, so be careful not to stray from the authorised paths.

Windyhaugh is notable on the long cul-de-sac up Coquetdale for having both a school and a telephone-box. Just under 1 mile (1.6km) from the hamlet the road crosses the bridge over the Rowhope Burn – the starting point.

Take the asphalted track that runs up the valley alongside the burn. At Rowhope Farm the stream divides, and the track follows the Trows Burn, the eastern tributary, up to the farmhouse, which takes its name from this watercourse. After the house, take the left-hand track **Ⓐ**, which passes through a ford, although there is also a footbridge.

There follows a steep climb to Trows Law, one of the few testing gradients on the route. On days when the army is not firing, the silence up here is over-

whelming – you will be unfortunate indeed if you hear a motor vehicle in the next three hours or so. The crows or 'hoodies' – birds hated by shepherds – fly in joyful exuberance, and the grass is springy underfoot. As you climb, the view becomes ever more spectacular behind you – a good excuse for pausing to catch breath. An army noticeboard reminds walkers that this is an army training-area. Do not pick up any strange objects. Continue on the track, even though this becomes less distinct. A grand array of summits comes into view ahead.

The track winds up to another military noticeboard **Ⓑ**. Bear to the left here and continue climbing, not forgetting to look back. At the top you come to a fence with a stile that leads to a

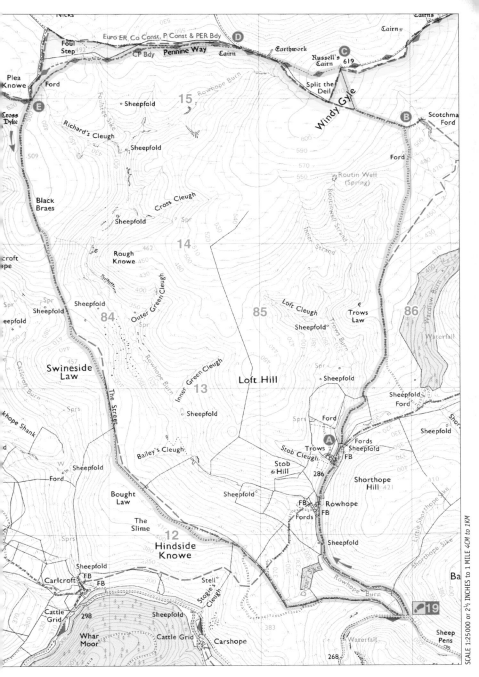

Nicks

Cairns

Foul Step

Euro ER, Co Const, P Const & PER Bdy **D**

Cairn

Plea Knowe

Ford

CP Bdy Pennine Way Cairn

Earthwork

Russell's Cairn **C** 619

Cross Dyle **E**

Sheepfold

15

Rowhope Burn

Split the Deil

Windy Gyle

Scotchma Ford

Richard's Cleugh

Sheepfold

B

Ford

Black Braes

Cross Cleugh

Sheepfold

Spr

600

590

570

550

Routin Well (Spring)

Ford

croft pe

Rough Knowe

462

14

Inner Strand

Routinwell Strand

Outer Green Cleugh

Swineside Law

84

Sheepfold

Sheepfold

eepfold

Spr

457

The Street

Inner Green Cleugh

13

85

Loft Cleugh

Sheepfold

Loft Hill

Trows Law

86

Waterfall

Wardlaw Burn

Carlcroft Burn

khope Shank

d

Sheepfold

Ford

Bailey's Cleugh

Bought Law

Sheepfold

Sheepfold

Spr

Ford

Trows

Stob Cleugh

Stob Hill

286

Fords Sheepfold FB

A

Sheepfold

Ford

Sheepfold

Shorthope Hill 421

Sho

The Slime

12

Hindside Knowe

FB

Fords

Rowhope FB

Sheepfold

Little Shorthope Sike

Shorthope Sike

Ba

Sheepfold FB

Carlcroft

FB

Stell

Stage's Cleugh

Sheepfold

Rowhope Burn

Dread no

19

Cattle Grid

298

Whar Moor

Sheepfold

Cattle Grid

Carshope

383

268

Waterfall

Sheep Pens

SCALE 1:25000 or 2½ INCHES to 1 MILE 4CM to 1KM

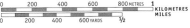

0	200	400	600	800 METRES	**1**
					KILOMETRES
					MILES
0	200	400	600 YARDS	½	

cairn **C** and triangulation pillar. This is Russell's Cairn, which bestrides the border between England and Scotland and is one of Britain's classic viewpoints. The actual cairn is prehistoric even though it takes its name from Lord

Francis Russell, who was killed here in 1585 at the side of his father-in-law, Sir John Forster, the Warden of the

Looking into Scotland from Russell's Cairn

Middle Marches, during a Wardens' Tryst or Meeting. There is said to have been a drovers' inn and even a cockpit up here at one time. The view extends far into the lowlands of Scotland – Sir Walter Scott's Eildon Hills being easily identified – while in other directions the soft curves of the Cheviot landscape stretch to a lonely infinity.

Russell's Cairn is on the route of the Pennine Way, which we now follow westwards with the fence on the left. It is a well-used path along the ridge. The Way is probably the most famous of Britain's long-distance footpaths. The route was first proposed in 1935 but was not opened until thirty years later. The original aim of the 250-mile (400km) route – to link 'the high places of solitude' – makes it as successful an expedition today as it was in the days of its conception. Near the bottom of a dip cross the fence by a stile and head uphill, following the fence ⓓ. Windy Rigg is to the right, while on the left are the headwaters of the various tributaries

of the Rowhope Burn, which seem to have their origins in the morass known as Foul Step. When the fence turns sharply right veer left on a path heading downhill to cross the boggy Foulstep Sike, then continuing along a well trodden path, crossing Richards Cleugh to reach a signpost and crossroads by a bridleway ⓔ.

Turn left onto the bridleway and continue along it with the steep drop to the Easthope Burn on the right, climbing Black Braes and then descending before climbing Swineside Law.

The views are a compensation for the climb, which is the last on this route. Follow the fence on the most used path down from here. This is the Street, an ancient drovers' way, which eventually reaches the bridge over the Rowhope Burn – the starting point of the walk, where one mystery remains. Close to the stream there is a signboard looking like a footpath indicator, however, it bears the legend 'Georgius 860115'. It is easy to muse on the reasons for this being here for the entire length of the drive home. ●

Cauldshiels Loch and the River Tweed

Start	Gun Knowe Loch, Tweedbank (on the eastern outskirts of Galashiels)
Distance	9½ miles (15.3km)
Approximate time	4 hours
Parking	At start
Refreshments	None on route
Ordnance Survey maps	Landranger 73 (Peebles, Galashiels & Selkirk), Explorer 337 (Peebles & Innerleithen) and 338 (Galashiels, Selkirk & Melrose)

The outward part of the route uses country lanes to climb into the hills to the south of the town. Cauldshiels Loch is a beauty spot that locals prefer to keep for themselves – it is a grand spot for a picnic. After this the climbing is done and the route follows a track along the crest of the hills. Another quiet road takes you down to a path along the banks of the River Tweed, which passes Abbotsford on its way back to Galashiels.

From the parking spaces by the side of the man-made loch (set in a recreational area) walk westwards to the large roundabout on the A6091. Walk across this to the Abbotsford road on the far side (B6360). Turn left **Ⓐ** at a telephone-box standing close to the entrance to Abbotsford's car park. Climb the shady lane, bearing left at a large cattle shed and turning sharply to the right at a road junction **Ⓑ** to climb a steep hill. However, this is a comparatively easy way to gain height and there are views to the left of the Tweed valley and the Eildon Hills.

At Abbotsmoss there is a small, picturesque loch. Turn right at the T-junction **Ⓒ** even though the road sign warns that this is a dead-end. The gradient is slightly easier now but a breather is still welcome. Use it to take in the view towards Melrose. The

surfaced road ends but a good track continues giving a fine vista to the right over Faldonside Loch to Gala Hill. You have to take a few steps down the track to the left to view Cauldshiels Loch **Ⓓ**. Its northern shore is wooded, and a path winds through the trees past a succession of lochside spots ideal for a picnic. Be careful not to disturb fishermen.

Resume climbing the track past Dod Plantation – mainly of beech trees. Cauldshiels Hill is to the left crowned with a prehistoric fort and a defensive earthwork that extends 2 miles (3.2km) or so to the south-east. A high broadcasting mast is a prominent landmark ahead, standing above the quaintly named Halfcrown Corner. However, it will be some time before this point is reached. The track swings left after passing a corrugated byre and a sheep-

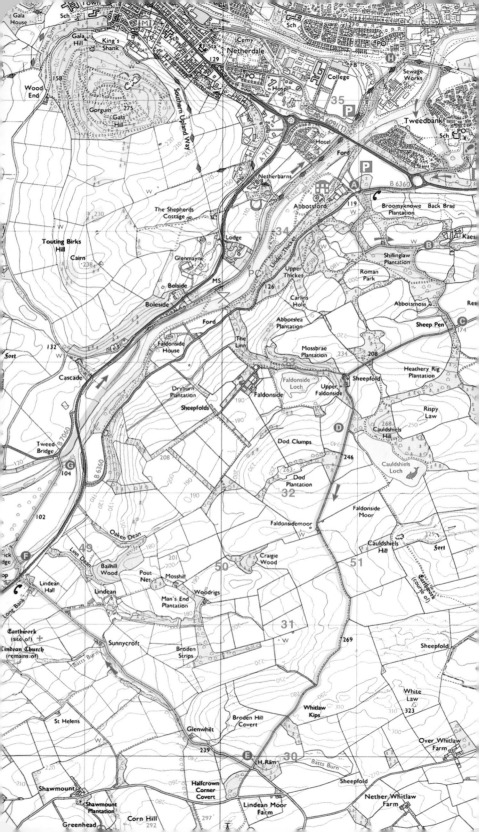

the riverside and a splendid viewpoint for Abbotsford, the home of Sir Walter Scott.

The path leads back to the road again, which goes underneath a high bridge. Keep to the riverside footpath and reach the road by a gasometer. Turn right following the Southern Upland Way sign and cross a bridge over Gala Water, the stream that was harnessed to power the woollen-mills to give Galashiels its prosperity in the mid-19th century. Turn right where electric lines overhang the road ⑪ to continue following the Southern Upland Way and cross a former railway bridge spanning the River Tweed. There is a good view of the Eildon Hills from here, and the river is well seen from this dizzy height. At the end of the bridge go down the steps by an electricity substation and walk along the path close to the riverbank, bearing right when it divides.

At the next fork go left to keep on the left-hand side of broad greensward. Cross a tarmac path to reach trees at the top. Gun Knowe Loch, the starting point, lies just beyond the trees, and you can reach the car park by walking round the loch in either direction. ●

fold and, after passing a gate secured by an unusual anchor device, it becomes grassy. This makes delightful walking with a fine view to the right, though this is later screened by a line of venerable hawthorns.

The descent to Halfcrown Corner begins by a wood. At the road ⑤ turn right to continue downhill to reach the valley of the River Tweed. The lane, though busier than the ones used earlier, is generally quiet enough and it will only take about 20 minutes to reach the main road. Cross the A7 and then the beautiful Ettrick Bridge ⑥, where the writer was fortunate in seeing a kingfisher. The route is now following the old course of the main road though the cat's-eyes have been removed and nettles are encroaching. The parkland of Sunderland Hall occupies the tongue of land between Ettrick Water and the Tweed, and the house may be glimpsed on the left through the fine trees.

Cross the Tweed Bridge ⑦ and descend the ramp immediately on the right to reach the riverside. Pass beneath the new bridge and enjoy the walking through the meadows by the broad river. Too soon the path joins a track that climbs from the riverside through trees and reaches a road. This leads to a picnic site where it is possible to walk by the river again. The road is rejoined near toilets, and soon after this (just beyond a road branching to the left) look for a waymarked path on the right, which leads to

Abbotsford

Grey Mare's Tail and Loch Skeen

Start	National Trust for Scotland car park at Grey Mare's Tail
Distance	6½ miles (10.5km)
Approximate time	4½ hours
Parking	Grey Mare's Tail
Refreshments	None
Ordnance Survey maps	Landranger 79 (Hawick & Eskdale), Explorer 37 (Pebbles & Innerleithen) and 338 (Galashiels, Selkirk & Melrose)

This is an energetic route with three steep climbs and some rough walking and boggy conditions in places. The steepest part comes right at the beginning along a well-constructed path beside the grand waterfall of the Grey Mare's Tail, before following the Tail Burn to the foot of the wild and lonely Loch Skeen. Then comes a circuit of the high ground around three sides of the loch, first climbing across rough, open moorland above its western shores to the magnificent viewpoint of Firthybrig Head, followed by a steep descent and then the third and final climb to Lochcraig Head. Finally, you descend along the eastern side to the foot of the loch again, here picking up your outward route. All the way there are extensive and impressive views over an austere landscape of rolling, empty hills. This walk should not be attempted in bad weather as route-finding could be difficult, especially in misty conditions.

Start by taking the stepped path on the right-hand side of the burn, signposted to Loch Skeen, that rises steeply above the Grey Mare's Tail to reach the top of the fall. This is the most strenuous part of the walk, however, from the path there are fine views of the waterfall. Continue along a rocky path above Tail Burn on the left through a rugged landscape eventually to emerge suddenly at the foot of Loch Skeen Ⓐ, which appears abruptly in its austere setting, cradled by surrounding steep hills.

Turn left to ford the burn at the outlet from the loch – there are plenty of large stones here. Then negotiate a boggy area on the far side and pick up a path through the heather that heads steeply up the hillside on the western side of the loch. Follow the path across the top, keeping away from the steep edge to the right, and continue in the same north-westerly direction, descending slightly

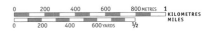

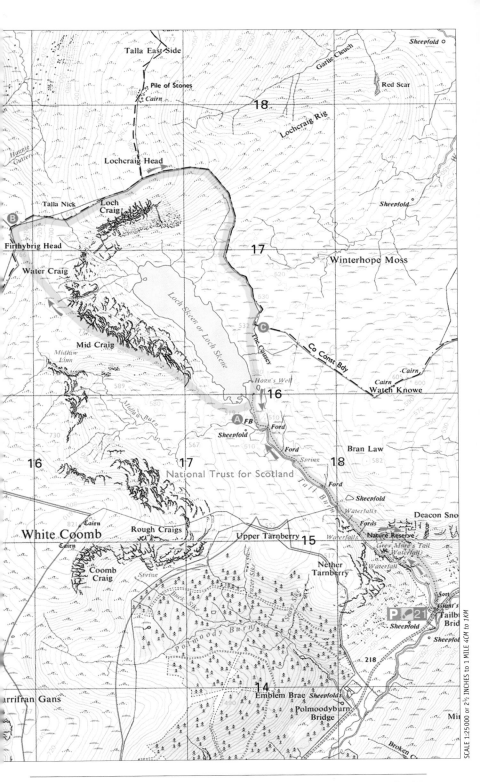

SCALE 1:25000 or 2½ INCHES to 1 MILE 4CM to 1KM

Talla East Side

Sheepfold

Garie Cleuch

Red Scar

Pile of Stones
Cairn

18

Lochcraig Rig

Lochcraig Head

Talla Nick

Loch
Craig

B

Sheepfold

Firthybrig Head

17

Winterhope Moss

Water Craig

Loch Skeen or Loch Skene

C

The Causey

Co Const Bdy

Mid Craig

Midlaw
Linn

Cairn

Watch Knowe

Cairn

589

Hom's Well

16

Midlaw Burn

A FB

Ford

Bran Law

Sheepfold

582

16

17

Ford

Ford

Spring

18

National Trust for Scotland

Ford

Sheepfold

730

567

510

Tail Burn

White Coomb

Cairn
Cairn

Rough Craigs

Upper Tarnberry

15

Waterfalls

Fords

Nature Reserve

Deacon Sno

Waterfalls

Grey Mare's Tail
Waterfall

Coomb
Craig

Spring

Nether
Tarnberry

Waterfall

Loch Skee

Polmoody Burn

P 21

Sheepfold

Tailb
Brid

Sheepfol

218

arrifran Gans

14

Emblem Brae

Sheepfolds

490

Polmoodyburn
Bridge

Broken C

Mi

and then climbing across open, rough, grassy moorland to reach a wall on Firthybrig Head Ⓑ. You should ideally aim to reach the wall where it bears right and another one joins it. From here there are magnificent and extensive views over the Border country, with Loch Skeen below.

Turn right alongside the wall, first heading down, then climbing steeply to Lochcraig Head, then descending steeply again. Keep beside the wall all the while, following it as it bends right and heads down towards the loch and taking care to avoid the wet, peaty sections. The wall later becomes a wire fence, and you keep beside it to where it turns left Ⓒ. At this point, head across the heather to the lochside and keep alongside it, picking up a discernible path, to reach the foot of the loch Ⓐ. Here you rejoin the outward route and retrace your steps to the starting point.

Grey Mare's Tail

Yearning Saddle and Deel's Hill

Start	Buckham's Bridge, 8 miles (12.9km) up the Coquet valley from Alwinton
Distance	7½ miles (12.1km)
Approximate time	4 hours
Parking	Car park at Buckham's Bridge
Refreshments	None
Ordnance Survey maps	Landranger 80 (Cheviot Hills & Kielder Water), Explorer OL16 (The Cheviot Hills)

The path by the lovely Blind Burn leads to the mountain shelter on Yearning Saddle, which is a welcome refuge for those trekking along the border ridge on the Pennine Way. There are seemingly infinite views into Scotland from the northern side of the ridge. The route then follows the Pennine Way south-westwards over lonely moorland to Brownhart Law – there are excellent views from here too – before heading back to the Coquetdale road over Deel's Hill to Buckham's Bridge. This is an invigorating highland walk without being too strenuous.

Turn left out of the car park and follow the road for just under ½ mile (800m) to Blindburn Bridge. Just before the bridge cross a stile to the left and head up the west side of the Blind Burn. Cross the stream over a plank bridge after 300 yds (274 m) and then continue on this side along and well trodden path. Dippers and herons will often be seen here. Since the creation of a new bridleway slightly west of here the use of this path by horses has ceased making it a much easier walk.

Cross the stream just after it is joined by another stream coming down from Gimmermoor Cairns and follow the path uphill to Yearning Hall **A**, the site of a ruinous croft surrounded by a few weather-beaten pines. The name 'Yearning' is said to derive from the

Anglo-Saxon *erne*, a word often given to soaring birds of prey. In the past this area is likely to have been the hunting-ground of white-tailed as well as golden eagles, though the latter are rarely seen

A view from Black Halls on the Pennine Way

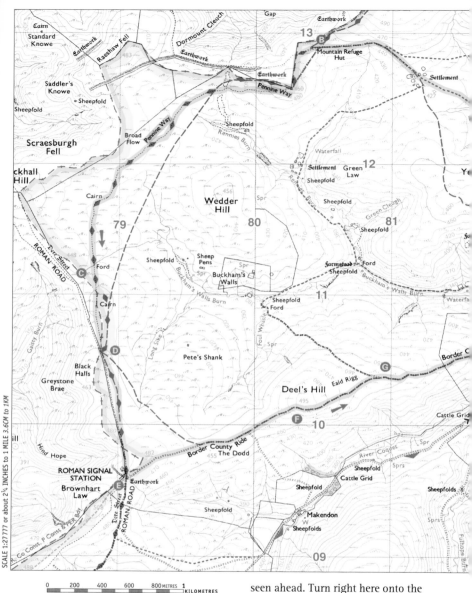

in the Cheviots today. The white-tailed
eagle became extinct in Britain about
seventy years ago.

Pass the ruined croft then veer right,
uphill, passing to the left of a green
shed. Cross a small stream to pick up a
more distinct footpath heading to the
left. Pass an ancient circular enclosure
from where a waymarker post should be
seen ahead. Turn right here onto the
bridleway, a well used track that winds
round to reach the mountain shelter at
Yearning Saddle **B**. There are superb
views from here if you step a few yards
into Scotland. The Kip is the summit
with a pyramid on top.

From the shelter keep on the
bridleway until it reaches the corner of
a fence. The Pennine Way now passes
over bleak moorland keeping the fence
at a short distance to the right. Keep

causeway **C**. After about an hour the path reaches Deer Street and the Border Ridge at Black Halls. There's a signpost here **D** with several options but keep on the Pennine Way and head south towards Chew Green.

After another ½ mile (800m), reach a signpost and leave the Pennine Way. Take the Bridleway to the left towards Deel Hill and Blindburn **E**. This is the Border County Ride and is well waymarked along its entire length. Unfortunately it is also well used by horses and can be exceedingly boggy particularly in wet weather.

Continue following this path to near the summit of Deel's Hill **F**. There's a superb view from here on a clear day. Keep straight ahead on the path from here to reach a waymarked junction **G**. The path to the left heads towards Buckham's Walls. Ignore this and keep straight ahead and eventually the boggy surface will give way to springy turf then reach a gate where you can cross by a stile. Head downhill from here passing by a black rock standing stone to reach the car park at Buckham's Bridge. ●

straight ahead at a crossroads with a waymarker and follow this boggy well used path to cross the head of the Buckham's Walls Burn on a stone

On Deel's Hill

Eccles Cairn and the College valley

Eccles Cairn and the College valley

Start	Hethpool
Distance	7½ miles (12.1km)
Approximate time	3½ hours
Parking	Small layby just before Hethpool on a left-hand bend where the road to Elsdonburn and Trowupburn goes through a gate straight ahead
Refreshments	None
Ordnance Survey maps	Landranger 74 (Kelso), Outdoor Leisure 16 (The Cheviot Hills)

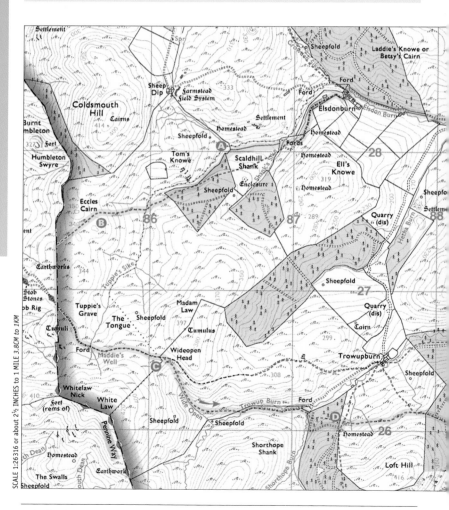

The College valley is one of the better-kept secrets of the Cheviots. A few permits each day are available from an estate agent in Wooler to motorists who wish to drive up to Mounthooly (it is an easy way to get up to the Pennine Way and the Cheviot) but it is an enjoyable road to walk, and this route explores a lonely tract of country by the border fence as well as the valley itself, which is particularly glorious mantled in autumn colour. Do not attempt this walk unless you are certain of good visibility.

Go through the gate ahead of you on the made-up track labelled to Elsdonburn and Trowupburn. Bear to the right when the road forks, heading towards a farm by the side of a wood. This farm – Elsdonburn – turns out to

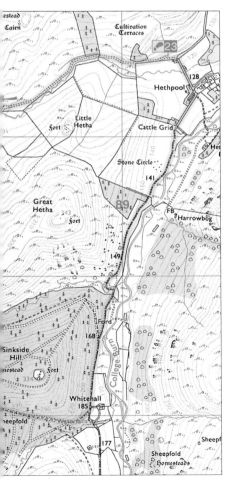

be a modern bungalow. Pass through the farmyard by walking to the left of the bungalow and follow the yellow waymark through a gate onto a rough track on the open hillside that winds towards plantations. The track dips down to cross Shank's Sike. Go through the gate here and head across the field, making for the gate Ⓐ at the lower corner of the right-hand planting of conifers.

Go through the gate and turn left so that you are following the left side of the wood, with a stream on the right. The small hut on the right is where shepherds would once have lived during lambing. In the distance a path can be seen climbing towards Eccles Cairn. The wood on the left is the home of noisy jays.

At the corner of the wood the path descends to a bridge across the stream. Standing here, you should see the first of a series of white-topped posts marking the path up to the cairn, which are a useful aid to navigation. From the final post the path bears to the right to reach the viewpoint, Eccles Cairn Ⓑ. On a good day this provides a magnificent panorama of the Scottish lowlands. The twin townships of Town Yetholm and Kirk Yetholm are just below: the finishing point of the Pennine Way according to Wainwright, who used to

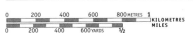

The Pennine Way near Eccles Cairn

A good track leads from these pens to Trowupburn. However, the right-of-way lies to the right, where a broken stile once took the path into the trees, but this route has been overgrown and replaced by another a little further to the south. Climb with the trees on the left to a point where spruces (Christmas trees) give way to pines with their darker bunches of needles. Here you should just be able to discern a steep path leading into the planting. Although it looks unlikely, it emerges into a broad firebreak with a good path. Now there are spruces on both sides.

This path comes out of the forest above Trowupburn ⒟. Turn to the left on emerging from the conifers to find a well-defined path a little lower down, which heads towards more trees on the other side of Loft Hill. This is a fine spot to photograph, with the small dwelling of the shepherd providing scale for a vast and lonely landscape.

A gate leads into the next, more extensive, tract of woodland. Pause to look back from here and you may see minute figures on the skyline trudging along the Pennine Way. The gate leads into a firebreak, which dips down steeply. Hare Law is the summit on the far side of the College valley, which is slowly revealed. The forest track reaches the valley road above Whitehall. Turn left to follow the road back to Hethpool. There are several lovely places where one can rest by the stream and take in the charm of this hidden beauty spot. The last stretch of the road runs through meadows to reach Hethpool, where the picturesque estate cottages have wonderfully colourful gardens. ●

leave a pint 'in salt' here for those stalwarts who managed to complete the route from start to finish. Since his death the measure has been reduced to half a pint, paid for by the brewery. Beyond the Yetholms the Eildon Hills can be seen in the distance, beloved of Sir Walter Scott.

Leave Eccles Cairn on a clear path leading to the south-west to reach the border fence – which is a wall here – and follow this southwards until the Pennine Way joins it through a gate – the signpost is on the Scottish side. Take the track to the left here.

The path skirts the head of a small burn, Maddies Well, and then follows the contours to reach a fence below Madam Law ⒞. From here the main path leads high up on the left side of the steep valley known as Wide Open. This is too easy. Leave this path early on to descend over rough ground to the bottom of the valley of the Trowup Burn, where there is a vague path on the left side. It eventually reaches a gate by a circular sheep-pen. Cross the stream here to reach a much broader, grassy path. This leads to more sheep-pens, which are passed on the left.

Hartside, Salter's Road and High Cantle

Start	Hartside, 6 miles (9.7km) west of A697, beyond Powburn and Ingram
Distance	8 miles (12.9km)
Approximate time	4½ hours
Parking	On the verge of public road before Hartside Farm
Refreshments	None
Ordnance Survey maps	Landranger 80 (Cheviot Hills & Kielder Water), Explorer OL16 (The Cheviot Hills)

This walk reveals one of the most enjoyable characteristics of the Cheviots – their loneliness. For much of it you have to strain your eyes to see signs of human occupation, if any is visible at all. Some of the way is on vague, heathery tracks made either by sheep or shooting parties. It is wise to take a compass and try the route only on a day of good visibility.

At Hartside take the farm road branching to the left, which leads to Alnhammoor. The River Breamish is soon on the right, forming a foreground for the lovely Cheviot landscape. At Alnhammoor cross the bridge, climb to the top of the incline and turn left before the house on a path waymarked as a permissive path. Turn sharply to the right at the end of this short path to pass behind the farmhouse **Ⓐ**.

The Shank Burn is now on the left. Keep to the lower path and cross the fence at a stile bearing a footpath waymark just beyond a stell (round sheepfold). Cross a streamlet, the Rowhope Burn, and follow the path up through tall bracken. At this point, frequent waymark posts show the line of the path to the open hillside. However, sheep using them as scratching posts sometimes uproot them from the shallow soil, and they are not always replaced with the arrows pointing in the correct direction. If in doubt about the path, climb gently in a south-westerly direction across the heathery waste until the view ahead opens up. Shank Burn should still be on your left. Head for the dip between the low, rounded Little Dod on the left – with the cairn on the summit of Hogdon Law visible beyond – and the lower slopes of Shill Moor to the right.

When the view opens up even more, the path continues heading south-westwards towards a black cattle-shelter, with a planting of pines on the saddle of Cushat Law beyond. It soon comes to the junction with Salter's Road **Ⓑ**; here the path carries straight on, in the direction shown by a blue bridleway waymark. The black cattle-shelter is now on the left.

Salter's Road took its name from its regular use by salt-traders who brought

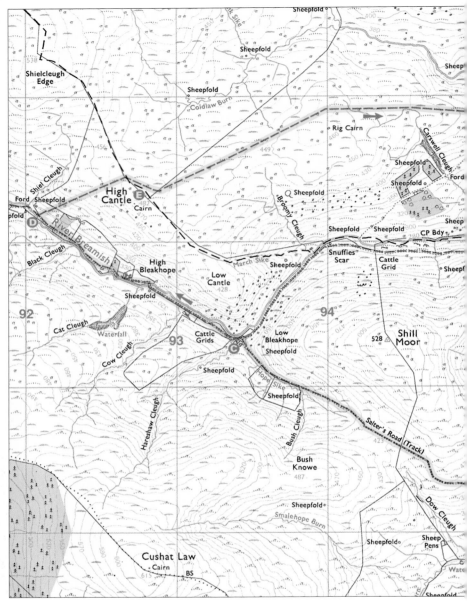

the precious commodity by this route from the salt-pans on the coast. In bygone days meat could be preserved only by smoking or salting, so salt was vital if folk were to have food other than grain in the winter. Salter's Road was also busy with drovers and their flocks and herds, and the route was used by whisky-smugglers too, who carted the liquor from illicit stills hidden in remote valleys to customers in the lowland villages and towns.

The initial climb on the road is steepish but it soon levels out in a broad valley. After a gate the view westwards opens up with Bleakhope far below. The rough path follows the Hope Sike; there is quite a drop on the left but this is an enjoyable part of the walk.

Anyone feeling fatigued at this point

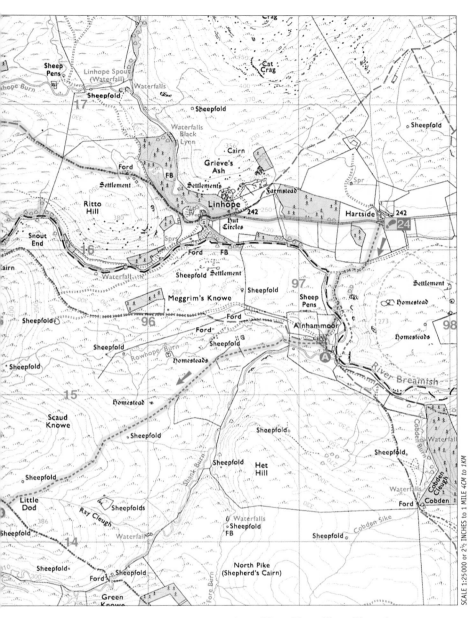

SCALE 1:25000 or 2½ INCHES to 1 MILE 4CM to 1KM

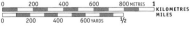

0   200   400   600   800 METRES   1

KILOMETRES
MILES

0   200   400   600 YARDS   ½

C could escape the rest of the walk by returning to Alnhammoor by the bridleway that follows the valley of the Breamish. But the walk continues by turning left at Low Bleakhope onto the farm road and following the stream up-river. Pass through a series of gates at High Bleakhope and follow the track past small wooded areas. Often there is a heron fishing in the Breamish here.

After another, larger clump of trees **D**, this time deciduous, climb by the fence – taking care over wet ground – to a gate at the top. Keep on climbing to reach the top of High Cantle **E**, where there is a miniature cairn and a stupendous view in every direction.

Cross the fence so that the one running north-east is on the left and head across the heather towards Rig Cairn, whose summit can be seen ahead below that of Great Standrop. There are twin rocky hummocks on the left and no trace of the right-of-way on the ground. Take care here as it is no place to injure an ankle.

From Rig Cairn the view eastwards is revealed. Head in this direction, using paths made by the vehicles of shooters where possible. At first make for the plantation to the left of the conical Ritto Hill and then, when you can see it, for the gateway where three fences meet. You now follow a blue waymark that leads to a decent track going to Linhope Wood. A path to the left climbs to the waterfall – Linhope Spout – but the final part of our route bears right to reach Linhope itself, from where the road descends to Hartside and back to the starting point.

The River Breamish near Hartside

Kirk Yetholm and the Halterburn valley

Start	Kirk Yetholm
Distance	8 miles (12.9km)
Approximate time	4½ hours
Parking	Around the green at Kirk Yetholm
Refreshments	Pub at Kirk Yetholm
Ordnance Survey maps	Landranger 74 (Kelso & Coldstream), Explorer OL16 (The Cheviot Hills)

To walkers Kirk Yetholm is principally known as the northern terminus of the Pennine Way, the finishing point for the majority of people who walk it from south to north. This walk uses the last few miles of the Pennine Way, the outward route following the 'High-Level Main Route' and the return route using the 'Low-Level Alternative Route'. It is a reasonably energetic walk with quite a lot of climbing – lengthy and steady rather than steep and strenuous – over the smooth, grassy slopes of the Cheviots with extensive views across a rolling and largely empty landscape. Regular waymarking and clear paths make it an easy route to follow, especially as part of it is beside the fence that marks the border between Scotland and England.

Begin by taking the lane, signposted to Halterburn, that leads off from the green. The lane winds uphill and then descends to cross a cattle-grid by a Pennine Way finger-post Ⓐ. Turn left to ford Halter Burn by another finger-post – after heavy rain it will be advisable to use the footbridge about 100 yds (91m) to the right – and head uphill by a wall on the left. Just before the wall ends, bear right to follow a path

The rolling, empty landscape of the Cheviots

SCALE 1:25000 or 2½ INCHES to 1 MILE 4CM to 1KM

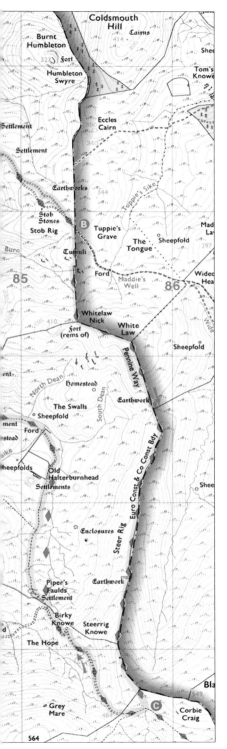

along the side of the valley across smooth, grassy slopes, keeping to the left of sheep-pens and heading up to Stob Rig.

On reaching a wall, bear right **B** to continue alongside it. Apart from a few descents into hollows, the next 2 miles (3.2km) are a virtually continuous uphill route that climbs several stiles and keeps beside the border fence – the double wire fence on the left that marks the border between Scotland and England – all the time across Stob Rig, White Law and Steer Rig. It is a magnificent ridge walk across an empty and open landscape, with fine views to the left over the Cheviots towards the Northumberland coast and to the right over the Scottish Border country with the three Eildon peaks prominent.

After you climb a ladder-stile, the border fence bears left, but you follow a path to the right to reach a junction of paths **C**, where the High-Level Main Route and the Low-Level Alternative Route meet. Turn sharp right onto the low-level route, go through a kissing-gate and then follow a winding path downhill. Go through another kissing-gate and continue to a ruined farm (Old Halterburnhead) near the first group of trees seen for a long while.

Here the Pennine Way turns left, becomes a track and continues through the valley above the burn.

At a farm (Burnhead), keep to the left of the farm buildings and turn right **D** through a metal gate to continue along the track. The track soon becomes a tarmac lane, and you follow this lane past Halterburn to rejoin the outward route and retrace your steps to Kirk Yetholm.

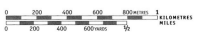

Craster, Howick and Longhoughton

Start	Craster
Distance	8 miles (12.9km). Shorter version 4½ miles (7.2km)
Approximate time	4 hours (2 hours for shorter version)
Parking	National Trust car park at Craster
Refreshments	Pubs and cafés at Craster and Longhoughton
Ordnance Survey maps	Landranger 81 (Alnwick & Morpeth), Explorer 332 (Alnwick & Amble)

Most people immediately head for Dunstanburgh Castle to the north of Craster (see Walk 7); this route provides a less-trodden alternative. Although the cliffs are low, the seascape is never dull and on a rough day may be spectacular. There are several beaches suitable for picnicking. For the most part the return is by quiet lanes and field paths. A shorter version of the walk is suggested.

Leave the car park by the footpath that goes towards the harbour parallel to the road, which is a little distance below. However, do not bear to the left past the tearoom towards the harbour but carry straight on, and at the road bear right, following a footpath sign to Howick (there is a beguiling glimpse of the Jolly Fisherman pub in front of you before you turn to the right).

The path goes behind houses, bungalows and then a school, formerly an outdoor centre but now disused. At this point there are fields on the right, and just beyond the school there is a footpath junction. Take the left fork, walking towards the sea, to join a path Ⓐ near the edge of the cliff going south. This is good walking on springy turf, while the waves beat on a rocky platform below. Note the jointing of the rock, which is typical of the Whin Sill extrusion. Behind, Dunstanburgh is in

view as far as Cullernose Point, then the intriguing gothic silhouette of a house on the shore at Howick gives interest to the view ahead. Note the contortion of the strata near Swine Den; the path is narrow here, close to the cliff edge. On the right the triangulation pillar on the top of Hips Heugh is clearly visible.

The footpath bears to the left just before the road, and there may be a slightly prickly interlude as it passes through undergrowth between the sea and the road. However, this is brief, and the path soon regains its position on the open top of the cliff.

The sinister house seen ahead for some time turns out to be ancient. Originally a fisherman's house, its masonry has been honeycombed by centuries of weathering.

Just beyond this, cliff erosion has forced the path away from the sea **B**. However, the old path is still walkable (and a right-of-way) for $^1/_4$ mile (400m), and this leads to a delightful picnic spot – the beach at Rumbling Kern – where an underwater passage has been eroded to create a large pool separated from the ocean which, on a rough day, looks like a natural jacuzzi. Note the inscription on the rock here: 'Ye Howick Camp', which flourished between 1902 and 1905.

Return from this delectable spot to take the lane that leads around Sea Houses Farm.

For the shorter walk, keep straight on down the road to reach the lodge of Howick Hall **F**, *then follow the route after* **F**.

Turn left at the end of the short, green lane and continue southwards after the farm, down a track that may be used only by pedestrians or disabled motorists. This field track soon reaches the seaside again at Howick Burn Mouth **C**. Here a graceful concrete footbridge arches over the little stream. Once you have climbed to the top of the hill, on the far side you will notice a change in the coastal scenery: the clifftop is lower and there are no rocks. When you come to a made-up road on the right **D**, follow it to reach Longhoughton.

The quiet lane reaches the village by the church. Turn left for a few yards if you wish to visit it, otherwise make a right turn at the village street, which, as the name implies, is lengthy. Pass the stores on the right, where a tearoom is open during the week, and the Burnside Inn on the left.

At the end of the village, where the road bends sharply left, take the footpath on the right **E** threading through the trees. After 200 yds (183m) turn left through a gate and follow the path on a broad headland between two crops towards a clump of trees. The path continues on the edge of the next field along another wide path. When you come to a lane, turn right and follow it through beautiful woodland, crossing a road bridge over the Howick Burn and then passing beneath another bridge, which takes an estate path over the road.

The road bends sharply to the right at the gatelodge to Howick Hall where the shorter route joins **F**. Keep straight on here; the footpath is right of the gate-lodge. The hall is the home of Lord Howick, a descendant of the 2nd Earl Grey, of Reform Bill fame, who lived here from 1801 to1845. The gardens are open to the public and are at their best in spring and early summer.

Beginning as a track, the right-of-way soon becomes a field path following the edge of the woods. The other side of Hips Heugh can now be seen on the right, a rocky crag screened by Scots pines. On the left there is a delightful cricket ground overlooked by a house optimistically called Peep O'Sea. At the end of the woods go through the gate and walk across a broad meadow to a stile. Over this, skirt Hips Heugh (still on the right) to reach a footpath junction **G** where a decision has to be made between two paths. That to the right returns to Craster via Howick Scar, which gives lovely views over the village to the castle. However it means retracing steps to make a back-yard entrance to Craster.

The route to the left is preferable, using a field path to Craster South Farm. Cross the road to a kissing-gate which leads to a path through a meadow towards the cliff-face of the quarry, half-screened by trees. At the corner of this meadow close to the trees there is a gate onto a lovely woodland path which leads directly into the car park at Craster. ●

Traquair and Minch Moor

Start	Traquair
Distance	10 miles (16.1km)
Approximate time	5 hours
Parking	By village hall at Traquair
Refreshments	None
Ordnance Survey maps	Landranger 73 (Peebles, Galashiels & Selkirk), Explorer 337 (Peebles & Innerleithen) and 338 (Galashiels, Selkirk & Melrose)

A steady climb along the ancient routeway of the Minchmoor Road, following part of the Southern Upland Way, leads to the summit of Minch Moor (1860ft/567m), a magnificent viewpoint over the Border country. This is followed by a descent through the conifers of Elibank and Traquair Forest and a walk through the pleasant valley of Bold Burn. The final leg is along a quiet lane below the forested slopes, partly beside the River Tweed. This is a superb combined hill, moorland and forest walk with splendid views but, despite clear and well-surfaced tracks throughout, not recommended in misty conditions.

The walk starts at the war memorial, where you follow the direction of a Southern Upland Way sign along a lane, passing the village hall on the left. Head uphill and, where the lane bends right, continue along the track ahead, signposted Minchmoor.

Follow the track, initially enclosed between walls, steadily uphill, climbing several stiles and going through a number of gates. There are grand views over the Tweed valley. Later the track enters the conifers of Elibank and Traquair

View from the route up Minch Moor

Forest and eventually emerges onto the open heathery expanses of Minch Moor. Look out for the Cheese Well by a small stream. A notice states that cattle-drovers used to drop pieces of cheese into the well to gain the favour of the fairies haunting this spot and thus guarantee a safe journey. Continue across the moor and, just before the next group of conifers, a track leads off to the right **A** gently uphill to the triangulation pillar and cairn on the summit of Minch Moor **B**. This brief detour is well worth while for the magnificent all-round view of the encircling hills.

Retrace your steps and turn right to continue along the Southern Upland Way. Descend gently to a crossing of tracks and here turn left **C** off the Minchmoor Road and Southern Upland Way to continue along a broad track that curves left through the forest, heading gently downhill. The track later bends right across the slopes of Bold Rig. On meeting another track, turn sharp right along it **D** to head gently downhill to a junction of tracks.

Here turn sharp left **E**, almost doubling back, along a track through the valley of Bold Burn, a pleasant route mainly along the left-hand edge of conifers, with fine views of the Tweed valley. At a fork, continue along the left-hand track, go through a gate and pass between Forestry Commission chalets to reach a lane **F**.

Turn left and follow the lane for nearly 3 miles (4.8km) back to the start, an attractive and relaxing finale, passing below some delightful sloping woodland on the left and later keeping above the Tweed on the right. Finally join the B709 for the last ¾ mile (1.2km) to Traquair. ●

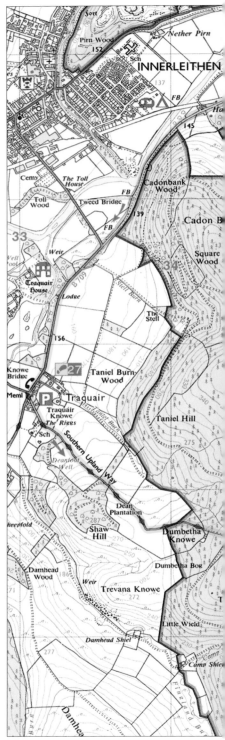

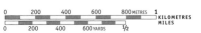

SCALE 1:25000 or 2½ INCHES to 1 MILE 4CM to 1KM

Around the Cheviot from Harthope valley

Around the Cheviot from Harthope valley

Start	The Harthope valley before Langleeford
Distance	12 miles (19.3km)
Approximate time	6½ hours
Parking	Off the road before Langleeford
Refreshments	None
Ordnance Survey maps	Landrangers 74 (Kelso & Coldstream) and 75 (Berwick-upon-Tweed), Explorer OL16 (The Cheviot Hills)

Gradients are rarely the problem in the Cheviots. The main cause of fatigue is likely to be the incessant wind, so choose a day of soft breezes and good visibility for this walk. Once on the border ridge, and if you still have the energy, it is comparatively easy to visit the summit of the Cheviot – allow an extra hour. Although there is about ¹/₂ mile (800m) of duckboarding after Auchope Cairn, there is still a lot of boggy ground after this, and it is hard to escape without at least one boot filled with peaty fluid. The return down to the Harthope valley is over rough ground, and once the side of the stream is reached the path is little better than a sheep-track.

Just before the wall that marks the boundary of the Langleeford property there is a narrow bridleway leaving the road to the right and waymarked to Broadstruther and Goldscleugh. The path follows the right bank of the Hawsen Burn, keeping fairly well up on the side of the valley but low enough to pass by a stell, or circular sheepfold, after the bridleway to Anstruther has branched to the right. Back across the Harthope valley, the summits of Housey and Langlee crags are distinctive landmarks, which are a welcome sight on the return leg of the route. They are tors, akin to those on Dartmoor, residues of hard volcanic rocks that forced their way to the surface from the

earth's core 380 million years ago.

Beyond the sheepfold the lower slopes of the valley of the Hawsen Burn are precipitous, and the faint path winds westwards above them, eventually arriving at a fence. Make for the gate in it **Ⓐ** and pass through it to begin descending into the pleasant valley ahead, heading for the bottom of the plantation on the right. The massive bulk of the Cheviot is on the left.

Cross a stile bearing a waymark at a gate near the lower end of the plantation into a broad, level windbreak. Follow the path to the western end of the wood; there is a thicket of tall, fragrant broom growing here. Go through this to a gate and then follow along the top of the plantation to a gateway at the end – watch out for adders on this path. Beyond this there is a faint path along the flank of the valley. This is soon joined by another path, which has followed the valley below the wood.

Keep on the right side of the stream towards Goldscleugh to join a track that goes through the 'inbye' land (the sheltered, relatively fertile enclosures of the valley bottom close to the farm). Cross the ford  – or the footbridge a little way upstream – and climb the track the short distance to the gate. After this, turn right to pass in front of the farmhouse. Cross another stream and keep outside the walls of the farmyard to pass to the right of a black corrugated metal building. Make for the gateway ahead, keeping below the slope with the birch trees. Turn left to the road.

A pleasant stretch follows on an even surface. There are views of the ravine below Dunsdale Crag. A footpath leaves the road on the left. Take this to cut off a corner towards the white-painted cottage of Dunsdale. Before the building, look to the left up the stream. This is the Bizzle Burn, which comes down from the top of the Cheviot through a steep ravine. Pass through the yard at Dunsdale to a gate by a black shed. Go through this and two more gates to reach the edge of a plantation. Turn left to follow its edge – this is excellent walking on a grassy path. As the way begins to drop towards Mounthooly the way ahead to the ridge looks forbidding. When the trees end there is a fine view of the Schill. Pass to the right side of the fence but continue to follow it. Cross the Braydon Burn and then go through the gate close to the stell to drop down to cross College Burn. There is a sort of rickety footbridge incorporated into the fence here. Having crossed the Burn, head up to the trees

The Cheviot from above Goldscleugh

and turn left onto a clear path B.

The path is easy to follow as far as Smeddum Sike D. Before the stell here make for the topmost plantation. Turn left again here to follow the fence, and then at the end of the somewhat stunted pines bear slightly to the right to begin the climb over rough ground to Red Cribs. The latter is a gash in the hillside, which should be passed on its right (north-west) side. The border fence is soon visible at the crest of the climb. Turn left to follow the Pennine Way eastwards E.

The mountain refuge hut is situated close to this point before the next challenge, which is the long climb to Auchope Cairn. The refuge offers shelter from the weather and a superb view of the surrounding heights. The Hen Hole, best seen from Auchope Cairn, is the awesome chasm from where music of magical sweetness is said to emanate, enticing the unwary to fall to its rocky depths. Sunshine never reaches these depths, and snow is said to linger on Midsummer Day.

The cairn itself F stands at a height of 2418ft (737m), just 256ft (78m) less than the Cheviot summit, and is surrounded by a sea of shattered rock. It is certainly a better viewpoint and one of the finest in England. Using binoculars

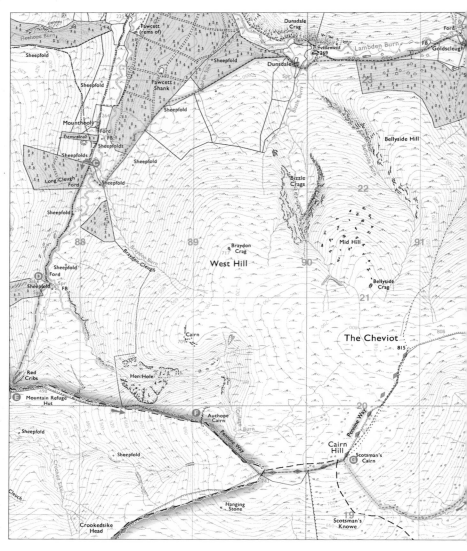

on a clear day, you are supposed to be able to identify the shape of Lochnagar, near Balmoral on Deeside, over 100 miles (160km) distant.

From Auchope Cairn the route continues south-eastwards along the Pennine Way over about ½ mile (800m) of duck-boarding. At the end of this there is a signpost. Bear left to follow the boggy footpath towards Cheviot summit. A line of old fencing posts marks the

route, which cuts across boggy ground to the north of the fence. When it meets the fence again, follow it to Scotsman's Cairn G. If you wish to visit the summit of the Cheviot, continue to follow the fence over boggy, though level, ground. This diversion will take at least an hour, so make sure you have time and energy enough to undertake it.

If you do not intend to make this diversion, or are returning from having made it, cross the fence by the stile and begin a descent over difficult ground towards the Harthope valley. The

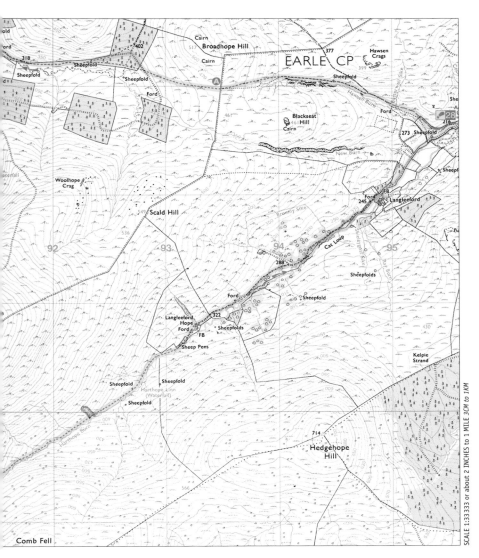

SCALE 1:33 333 or about 2 INCHES to 1 MILE 3CM to 1KM

direction is south-east, that is at right angles to the fence behind the cairn. After a few paces in this direction the head of the Harthope valley is obvious below. Take great care in descending over the tussocky grass as it would be unwise to sprain an ankle here. The water flowing from the innumerable springs on this slope has a delicious sweetness and purity.

At the bottom, a faint path follows the embryonic stream, crossing from side to side at first. After a while it settles for its left bank, and the stream grows from a trickle to a splash. The path becomes better defined as well. Harthope Linn is a beautiful waterfall contained in a shady dell.

Pass to the right of the sheep-pens at Langleeford Hope. Ford the stream and pass behind the house to join the track down the valley. From here the walking is fairly restful, but also pretty with Housey Crag and the mesa-like Langlee Crag landmarks. After Langleeford the road is made-up and runs by the inbye land of the farm. It soon reaches the Hawsen Burn and the starting point. ●

Further Information

 The National Parks and Countryside Recreation

Ten national parks were created in England and Wales as a result of an Act of Parliament in 1949. In addition to these, there are numerous specially designated Areas of Outstanding Natural Beauty, Country and Regional Parks, Sites of Special Scientific Interest and picnic areas scattered throughout England, Wales and Scotland, all of which share the twin aims of preservation of the countryside and public accessibility and enjoyment.

John Dower, whose report in 1945 created their framework, defined a national park as 'an extensive area of beautiful and relatively wild country in which, for the nation's benefit and by appropriate national decision and action, (a) the characteristic landscape beauty is strictly preserved, (b) access and facilities for public open-air enjoyment are amply provided, (c) wildlife and buildings and places of architectural and historic interest are suitably protected, while (d) established farming use is effectively maintained'.

Proposals for the creation of areas of protected countryside were first made before World War I, but nothing was done. The growing demand for access to open country and the reluctance of landowners – particularly those who owned large expanses of uncultivated moorland – to grant it led to a number of ugly incidents, in particular the mass trespass in the Peak District in 1932, when ramblers and gamekeepers came to blows and some trespassers received stiff prison sentences.

It was after World War II that calls for countryside conservation and access came to fruition in parliament. The National Parks and Countryside Act of 1949 provided for the designation and preservation of areas both of great scenic beauty and of particular wildlife and scientific interest throughout Britain. More specifically it provided for the creation of national parks in England and Wales.

Scotland was excluded because, with greater areas of open space and a smaller population, there were fewer pressures on the Scottish countryside.

A National Parks Commission, a forerunner of the Countryside Commission, was set up, and over the next eight years ten areas were designated as parks; seven in England (Northumberland, Lake District, North York Moors, Yorkshire Dales, Peak District, Exmoor and Dartmoor) and three in Wales (Snowdonia, Brecon Beacons and Pembrokeshire Coast). In 1989 the Norfolk and Suffolk Broads were added to the list. At the same time the Commission was also given the responsibility for designating other smaller areas of high recreational and scenic qualities (Areas of Outstanding Natural Beauty), plus the power to propose and develop long-distance footpaths, now called National Trails.

The authorities who administer the individual national parks have the very difficult task of reconciling the interests of the people who live and earn their living within them with those of visitors. National parks are not living museums and there is pressure to exploit the resources of the area, through more intensive farming, or through increased quarrying and forestry, extraction of minerals or the construction of reservoirs.

In the end it all comes down to a question of balance – between conservation and 'sensitive development'. On the one hand there is a responsibility to preserve the natural beauty of the national parks and to promote their enjoyment by the public, and on the other, the needs and well-being of the people living and working in them have to be borne in mind.

 The National Trust

Anyone who likes visiting places of natural beauty and/or historic interest has cause to be grateful to the National Trust. Without it, many such places would probably have vanished.

It was in response to the pressures on the countryside posed by the relentless march of Victorian industrialisation that the trust was set up in 1895. Its founders, inspired by the common goals of protecting and conserving Britain's national heritage and widening public access to it, were Sir Robert Hunter, Octavia Hill and Canon Rawnsley: respectively a solicitor, a social reformer and a clergyman. The latter was particularly influential. As a canon of Carlisle Cathedral and vicar of Crosthwaite (near Keswick), he was concerned about threats to the Lake District and had already been active in protecting footpaths and promoting public access to open countryside. After the flooding of Thirlmere in 1879 to create a large reservoir, he became increasingly convinced that the only effective way to guarantee protection was outright ownership of land.

The purpose of the National Trust is to preserve areas of natural beauty and sites of historic interest by acquisition, holding them in trust for the nation and making them available for public access and enjoyment. Some of its properties have been acquired through purchase, but many of the Trust's properties have been donated. Nowadays it is not only one of the biggest landowners in the country, but also one of the most active conservation charities, protecting 581,113 acres (253,176 ha) of land, including 555 miles (892km) of coastline, and over 300 historic properties in England, Wales and Northern Ireland. (There is a separate National Trust for Scotland, which was set up in 1931.)

Furthermore, once a piece of land has come under National Trust ownership, it is difficult for its status to be altered. As a result of parliamentary legislation in 1907, the Trust was given the right to declare its property inalienable, so ensuring that in any subsequent dispute it can appeal directly to parliament.

As it works towards its dual aims of conserving areas of attractive countryside and encouraging greater public access

Thirlwall Castle

(not easy to reconcile in this age of mass tourism), the Trust provides an excellent service for walkers by creating new concessionary paths and waymarked trails, maintaining stiles and foot bridges and combating the ever-increasing problem of footpath erosion.

For details of membership, contact the National Trust or the National Trust for Scotland at the addresses on page 94.

The Ramblers' Association

No organisation works more actively to protect and extend the rights and interests of walkers in the countryside than the Ramblers' Association. Its aims are clear: to foster a greater knowledge, love and care of the countryside; to assist in the protection and enhancement of public rights of way and areas of natural beauty; to work for greater public access to the countryside; and to encourage more people to take up rambling as a healthy, recreational leisure activity.

It was founded in 1935 when, following the setting up of a National Council of Ramblers' Federations in 1931, a number of federations earlier formed in London, Manchester, the Midlands and elsewhere came together to create a more effective pressure group, to deal with such problems as the disappearance and obstruction of footpaths, the prevention of access to open mountain and moorland and increasing hostility from landowners. This was the era of the mass trespasses, when there were sometimes violent confrontations between ramblers and gamekeepers, especially on the moorlands of the Peak District.

Since then the Ramblers' Association has played an influential role in preserving and developing the national footpath network, supporting the creation of national parks and encouraging the designation and waymarking of long-distance routes.

Our freedom to walk in the countryside is precarious and requires constant vigilance. As well as the perennial problems of footpaths being illegally obstructed, disappearing through lack of use or extinguished by housing or road construction, new dangers can spring up at any time.

It is to meet such problems and dangers that the Ramblers' Association exists and represents the interests of all walkers. The address to write to for information on the Ramblers' Association and how to become a member is given on page 94.

■ Walkers and the Law in England and Scotland

England (and Wales)

The following comments are intended simply as a helpful guide, backed up by the Countryside Access Charter, a concise summary of walkers' rights and obligations drawn up by the Countryside Commission, now the Countryside Agency.

There are three main kinds of public rights of way: footpaths (for walkers only), bridleways (for walkers, riders on horseback and pedal cyclists) and byways (used by all traffic). All these are shown by broken green lines on Ordnance Survey Outdoor Leisure, Explorer and Pathfinder maps, and by broken red lines on Landranger maps.

The term 'right of way' means exactly what it says. It gives right of passage over what, in the vast majority of cases, is private land, and you are required to keep to the line of the path and not stray on to the land on either side. Obstructions can sometimes be a problem and these and any other problems you encounter while on a walk should be reported to the rights-of-way department of the relevant council, which will take action with the landowner concerned.

Apart from the legal rights of way, there are certain other paths available for walkers. Many permissive or concessionary paths have been created where a landowner has given permission for the public to use a particular route across his land. Many of these routes are in country parks or on land owned by the Forestry Commission and National Trust. Walkers generally also have access to canal towpaths, most beaches and some areas of open and uncultivated land, such as the higher land of mountain, moorland and fell. On all permissive routes it is best to seek advice if at all unsure about access.

Scotland

The situation in Scotland is rather different than elsewhere in Britain.

It is sometimes said that there is no law of trespass in Scotland. In fact there is, but the trespass itself is not usually a criminal offence, and on open, hilly country there has in practice been a long tradition of free access for recreational walking – something both the Scottish Landowners' Federation and the Mountaineering Council of Scotland do not want to see changed. As evidence of this, an agreement – 'Scotland's Hills and Mountains: a Concordat on Access' – was published in 1996 between a wide range of farming, rambling, landowning, sports and outdoor organisations.

The watchdog on rights of way is the Scottish Rights of Way Society who maintain details on all established cases and will, if need be, contest attempted closures. The society also signposts many rights of way. Unlike England and Wales, rights of way are not marked on Ordnance Survey maps in Scotland and therefore a path on a map is no indication of a right of way. Many paths and tracks used by walkers were built by estates as stalking-tracks or

Countryside Access Charter

Your rights of way are:

- public footpaths – on foot only. Sometimes waymarked in yellow
- bridleways – on foot, horseback and pedal cycle. Sometimes waymarked in blue
- byways (usually old roads), most 'roads used as public paths' and, of course, public roads – all traffic has the right of way

Use maps, signs and waymarks to check rights of way. Ordnance Survey Explorer and Landranger maps show most public rights of way

On rights of way you can:

- take a pram, pushchair or wheelchair if practicable
- take a dog (on a lead or under close control)
- take a short route round an illegal obstruction or remove it sufficiently to get past

You have a right to go for recreation to:

- public parks and open spaces – on foot
- most commons near older towns and cities – on foot and sometimes on horseback
- private land where the owner has a formal agreement with the local authority

In addition you can use the following by local or established custom or consent, but ask for advice if you are unsure:

- many areas of open country, such as moorland, fell and coastal areas, especially those in the care of the National Trust, and some commons
- some woods and forests, especially those owned by the Forestry Commission
- country parks and picnic sites
- most beaches
- canal towpaths
- some private paths and tracks Consent sometimes extends to horse-riding and cycling

For your information:

- county councils and London boroughs maintain and record rights of way, and register commons
- obstructions, dangerous animals, harassment and misleading signs on rights of way are illegal and you should report them to the county council
- paths across fields can be ploughed, but must normally be reinstated within two weeks
- landowners can require you to leave land to which you have no right of access
- motor vehicles are normally permitted only on roads, byways and some 'roads used as public paths'

Further Information

for private access and although you may traverse such paths, taking due care to avoid damage to property and the natural environment, you should obey restricted access notices and leave if asked to do so.

Scotland likes to keep everything as natural as possible, so, for instance, waymarking is kept to a minimum. People are asked to 'walk softly in the wilderness, to take nothing except photographs, and leave nothing except footprints' – which is better than any law.

Safety on the Hills

The hills, mountains and moorlands of Britain, though of modest height compared with those in many other countries, need to be treated with respect. Friendly and inviting in good weather, they can quickly be transformed into wet, misty, windswept and potentially dangerous areas of wilderness in bad weather. Even on an outwardly fine and settled summer day, conditions can rapidly deteriorate. In winter, of course, the weather can be even more erratic and the hours of daylight are much shorter.

Therefore it is advisable to always take both warm and waterproof clothing, sufficient nourishing food, a hot drink, first-aid kit, torch and whistle. Wear suitable footwear, i.e. strong walking boots or shoes that give a good grip over rocky terrain and on slippery slopes. Try to obtain a local weather forecast and bear it in mind before you start. Do not be afraid to abandon your proposed route and return to your starting point in the event of a sudden and unexpected deterioration in the weather. Do not go alone. Allow enough time to finish the walk well before nightfall.

Most of the walks described in this book do not venture into remote wilderness areas and will be safe to do, given due care and respect, at any time of year in all but the most unreasonable weather. Indeed, a crisp, fine winter day often provides perfect walking conditions, with firm ground underfoot and a clarity that is not possible to achieve in the other seasons of the year. A few walks, however, are suitable only for reasonably fit and experienced hill-walkers able to use a compass and should definitely not be tackled by anyone else during the winter months or in bad weather, especially high winds and mist. These are indicated in the general description that precedes each of the walks.

Useful Organisations

Association for the Protection of Rural Scotland
Gladstone's Land, 3rd floor,
483 Lawnmarket, Edinburgh EH1 2NT.
Tel. 0131 225 7012

Council for National Parks
246 Lavender Hill,
London SW11 1LJ.
Tel. 020 7924 4077

Council for the Protection of Rural England
25 Buckingham Palace Road,
London SW1W 0PP.
Tel. 020 7976 6433

Countryside Agency
John Dower House, Crescent Place,
Cheltenham, Gloucs GL50 3RA.
Tel. 01242 521381

Forestry Commission
Information Branch,
231 Corstorphine Road,
Edinburgh EH12 7AT.
Tel. 0131 334 0303

Historic Scotland
Longmore House, Salisbury Place,
Edinburgh EH9 1SH.
Tel. 0131 668 8600

Long Distance Walkers' Association
Bank House, High Street,
Wrotham, Seven Oaks
Kent TN15 7AE
Tel. 01732 883705

National Trust
Membership and general enquiries:
PO Box 39, Bromley, Kent BR1 3XL.
Tel. 020 8315 1111
Northumbria Regional Office:
Scots' Gap, Morpeth NE61 4EG.
Tel. 01670 774691

National Trust for Scotland
28 Charlotte Square,
Edinburgh EH2 4ET.
Tel. 0131 243 9300

Northumberland National Park
Eastburn, South Park,
Hexham NE46 1BS.
Tel. 01434 605555; Fax 600522
*National Park Authority information centres (*not open all year):*
*Once Brewed: 01434 344396
Ingram: 01665 578248
*Rothbury: 01669 620424

Northumbrian Water
Kielder Water Tower Knowe Visitor Centre,
Falstone. Tel. 01434 240398

Ordnance Survey
Romsey Road, Maybush,
Southampton SO16 4GU.
Tel. 08456 05 05 05 (Lo-call)

Ramblers' Association (main office)
2nd Floor, Camelford House,
87–90 Albert Embankment,
London SE1 7TW
Tel. 020 7339 8500

Ramblers' Association (Scotland)
Kingfisher House,
Old Mart Business Park,

Milnathort, Kinross KY13 9DA.
Tel. 01577 861222

Scottish Natural Heritage
12 Hope Terrace, Edinburgh EH9 2AS.
Tel. 0131 447 4784

Scottish Rights of Way Society
17 Jock Lodge,
Edinburgh
Tel. 0131 652 2937

Tourist information:
Northumbria Tourist Board
Aykley Heads, Durham DH1 5UX.
Tel. 0191 375 3000
Scottish Borders Tourist Board
Shepherds Mills, Whinfield Road,
Selkirk TD7 5DT.
(For general information ring
Jedburgh below.)
*Tourist information centres (*not open
all year):*
Alnwick: 01665 510665
Bellingham: 01434 220616
Berwick-upon-Tweed: 01289 330733
*Coldstream: 0870 6080404
*Corbridge: 01434 632815
*Craster: 01665 576007
*Galashiels: 01896 75551
Haltwhistle: 01434 322002
Hexham: 01434 652220
*Jedburgh: 01835 863435/863688
*Kelso: 0870 6080404
*Melrose: 0870 6080404
Morpeth: 01670 500700
Newcastle upon Tyne: 0191 261 0610
*Peebles: 0870 6080404
Prudhoe: 01661 833144
*Seahouses: 01665 720884
*Selkirk: 01750 20054
*Wooler: 01668 281602

Youth Hostels Association
Trevelyan House, Dimple Road
Matlock, Derbyshire
DE4 3YH
Tel. 01629 592600
Scottish Youth Hostels Association
7 Glebe Crescent, Stirling FK8 2JA.
Tel. 01786 891400

Weather forecasts:
Scotland 7-day forecast. Tel. 0891 112260
UK 7-day forecast. Tel. 0891 333123

 *Ordnance Survey Maps
for Northumberland, the
Borders and Hadrian's Wall*
The area is covered by Ordnance Survey
1:50 000 scale (1$\frac{1}{4}$ inches to 1 mile or
2cm to 1km) Landranger map sheets 66,
67, 73, 74, 75, 79, 80, 81, 86, 87 and 88.
These all-purpose maps are packed with
information to help you explore the
area and show viewpoints, picnic sites,
places of interest and caravan and
camping sites.

To examine Northumberland, the
Borders and Hadrian's Wall in more detail,
and especially if you are planning walks,
Ordnance Survey Explorer maps OL16
(The Cheviot Hills), OL42 (Kielder Water &
Forest) and OL43 (Hadrian's Wall) at
1:25 000 scale (2$\frac{1}{2}$ inches to 1 mile or 4cm
to 1km) are ideal.

To get to the area use the Ordnance
Survey Great Britain Routeplanner Map at
1:625 000 scale (1 inch to 10 miles or 1cm
to 6.25km).

Ordnance Survey maps and guides are
available from most booksellers, stationers
and newsagents.

www.totalwalking.co.uk

www.totalwalking.co.uk
is the official website of the Jarrold
Pathfinder and Short Walks guides. This
interactive website features a wealth of
information for walkers – from the latest
news on route diversions and advice from
professional walkers to product news,
free sample walks and promotional offers.